TRANSFORM DRUG POLICY FOUNDATION

OUR MISSION:

Transform exists to reduce harm and pr
bringing about a just and effective syst
national and international levels

OUR ACTIVITIES:

- Research, policy analysis and innovative policy development
- Challenging government to demonstrate rational, fact-based evidence to support its policies and expenditure
- Promoting alternative, evidence-based policies to parliamentarians and government agencies
- Advising non-governmental organisations whose work is affected by drugs
- Providing an informed, rational and clear voice in the public and media debate on UK and international drug policy

OUR VISION:

- Social justice: restoration of human rights and dignity to the marginalised and disadvantaged, and regeneration of deprived neighbourhoods
- Reduced social costs: an end to the largest cause of acquisitive crime and street prostitution, and consequent falls in the non-violent prison population
- Reduced serious crime: dramatic curtailment of opportunities and incentives for organised and violent crime
- Public finances: the financial benefits of discontinued drug enforcement expenditure and the taxation of regulated drugs
- Public health: creation of an environment in which drug use can be managed and drug users can lead healthier lives
- Ethics: adherence to ethical standards and principles, including fair trade, in the manufacture, supply and distribution of drugs
- Reduced war and conflict: an end to the illegal drug trade's contribution to conflict and political instability in producer and transit countries

CONTENTS

FOREWORD

Transform has spent ten years drawing public attention to the failures of prohibition and the urgent need to replace it with a system of legal regulation, honing the arguments in the crucible of debate. Correctly applied, the ideas in this guide have the power to bring about truly transformational change across the world. It shows, for the first time, how to conceptualise and articulate the arguments for reform in such a way that they are unassailable. It will give you the tools and the facts to toughen your mind, to challenge prohibitionist misinformation, win over detractors and build the momentum for change in any debating arena you enter.

FROM DENIAL TO ACCEPTANCE

There is a well-recognised five-stage process that many go through in response to receiving catastrophic news – Denial, Anger, Bargaining, Depression, and Acceptance. In this case the catastrophe is the realisation that a 'drug-free world' is not going to happen and, worse, that our seemingly intractable 'drug problem' is to a large extent a self-inflicted nightmare. Modern policy making is frozen in the opening stages of denial and anger, creating a climate that is intensely hostile to attempts to adjust to the new environment and reinvest in the new reality. This guide is intended as a drug policy debating manual for those willing to undertake the journey from denial to reinvestment and then to help guide others through the process.

TWO LEVELS OF DEBATE

Anyone entering this debate must recognise that it operates on two very distinct levels. The first is the rational evidence-based discussion about what works and what does not, scientifically evaluating the outcomes of different policy options and making rational decisions based on that analysis. The second is the one governed by political considerations and priorities, the kind of debate seen when senior politicians enter the ring. These considerations range from international issues relating to UK and US foreign policy, to appealing to emotive and populist ideas: typically, an overriding need to appear 'tough on drugs' (or avoid appearing 'soft on drugs'). When

"The soft minded man always fears change. He feels security in the status quo, and he has an almost morbid fear of the new. For him the greatest pain is the pain of a new idea...There is little hope for us until we become tough minded enough to break loose from the shackles of prejudice, half truths and downright ignorance... A nation or a civilisation that continues to produce soft minded men purchases its own spiritual death on an instalment plan."

MARTIN LUTHER KING – 'STRENGTH TO LOVE'

the debate moves to this level, evidence is all too often jettisoned in favour of macho posturing and rhetoric, spin and sound bites.

In this political arena a virulent disease known as 'Green Room Syndrome' is epidemic, where strongly held beliefs on reform disappear as soon as the record button is pressed for broadcast. This is something we have experienced again and again: fellow-debaters who privately admit to agreeing with us in the Green Room before a media interview, only to feign shock and outrage at our position once the cameras and microphones are on. There are many in politics and public life who understand intellectually that the prohibition of drugs is unsustainable, but who default in public to moral grandstanding and emotive appeals to the safety of their children.

A RIGHTEOUS STANCE

It does not require courage to call for reform. Using the information in this booklet you will find that sound principles combined with imagination (and a little bit of factual homework) are quite sufficient to negotiate your way successfully through any debate. You can be assured that you are standing in very distinguished company, as the quotes scattered throughout this guide demonstrate. Don't be afraid of articulating the values that underlie your position and never concede the moral high ground. The drug policy debate need not be a battleground for entrenched and opposed ideologies; it can become an arena from which we can develop the momentum to make the world a better place. Drug policy reform is a principled and necessary step to enable us to address underlying issues of global poverty, marginalisation and freedom. Anyone arguing for drug policy reform is arguing with the evidence firmly on their side, and taking a righteous stance on an issue that has the power to effect a transformational, and hugely beneficial, paradigm shift in domestic and world politics.

DANNY KUSHLICK
BRISTOL
JULY 2007

INTRODUCTION

ABOUT THIS GUIDE

This is a guide to making the case for drug policy and law reform from a position of confidence and authority. It is based on Transform's experience in the public arena over the past ten years. In that time we have discussed and debated drug policy with Anne Widdecombe, Daily Mail columnists and The Drugs Tsar (UK and US versions), as well as Mayors, MPs, Ministers and even the Prime Minister. We have been grilled by Select Committees and Advisory Councils, by Jeremy Paxman and John Snow, by the Conservatives and the Lib-Dems, Greens and Socialists. We have given talks in the Home Office, at universities, to union meetings, mothers' groups, prison workers, drugs workers, magistrates, civil servants, the police, drug users and bereaved parents, and as far afield as Brussels, Athens, Seattle, Vancouver, LA and Belfast. There's a place for modesty, but it's not here – we really do know what we are talking about.

THIS GUIDE AIMS TO DO THREE THINGS:

- Reframe the debate by moving it away from polarised ideological positions and putting it squarely in the arena of rational, evidence-based policy thinking
- Provide the analytical framework and language to challenge entrenched prohibitionist policy positions with confidence and clarity, and to put forward the case for alternative policies including legally regulated drug markets
- Guide you to the facts you will need to support this progressive policy position

It is essentially all Transform's 'secrets' learnt on the front line of the drug debate, and we hope it will provide the tools for individuals in the public or policy arenas to take the debate forward towards real reform of policy and law in the coming months and years. The structure of the guide seeks to provide a narrative thread.

- Explaining the fault lines in the debate and the different mindsets that generate them
- Showing how these fault lines are often misunderstandings that can easily be bridged. Once common ground is established, it becomes possible to transcend the polarisation and confrontation that has dogged the debate and held back reform
- Demonstrating how the common ground - drug policy aims and principles on which both sides can agree - can be used as the basis for a rational and fundamental critique of prohibition
- Showing how to continue this analysis into making the case for legally regulated drug production and supply
- Showing how to respond to the most common concerns about moves towards legally regulated drug markets

This guide is aimed at people in government and civil society who understand that prohibition has been disastrously counter-productive and appreciate the need for an alternative, but who lack the analysis, facts or language tools to engage in the public debate with real confidence.

> "Some argue that, with the battle against drug-linked gun crime costing millions of pounds and many lives...the only solution is to legalise all drugs. That argument is yet to be resolved....... we are long way from even having an informed debate on this most explosive of issues."
>
> DAILY MAIL LEADER EDITORIAL – 30.12.03

Inevitably this short guide cannot provide all the answers; you will need to tailor your approach and use elements of the guide selectively for different audiences. What it aims to provide is a basic framework and tools that can be adapted to most scenarios you are likely to encounter. At the end we have provided detailed references and links to further information.

Please give us feedback on this document and let us know about your experiences in public debate, so that we can develop and improve it for future editions.

WHERE ARE WE UP TO TODAY?

The cause of drug law reform has been a prolonged struggle that began as soon as drug prohibition in its modern form came into being. Although prohibitions of various drugs stretch back into the 18th century (see Transform's history of prohibition timeline[1]), the modern drug law reform movement began in earnest with the social movements of the 1960s. It was during this decade that the 1961 UN Convention on Drugs enshrined prohibition as a truly global policy, and recreational drug use in the West simultaneously began its dramatic rise toward current levels.

The drugs debate has moved on considerably since that time, with the political, social and cultural landscape shifting and evolving dramatically, both in the UK and in the wider world. All the problems associated with drug prohibition and illegal markets have continued to worsen over the past four decades: the prevalence of illegal drug use has risen steadily despite the many billions spent on enforcing a policy intended to eradicate it. As prohibition's policy outcomes have deteriorated, the volume of calls for a rethink and serious consideration of alternative policy options has grown. This growth accelerated particularly rapidly during the 1990s as recreational use of illegal drugs became a truly mainstream youth phenomenon, and problematic use (of heroin in particular) ballooned to epidemic proportions. Problematic drug use now causes a level of secondary crime-related harms to wider society that is unprecedented in modern history, and was entirely unanticipated when drugs were prohibited.

It is now clear that our drug policy cannot continue down the same failed path forever. Prohibition's failure is now widely understood and acknowledged among key stakeholders in the debate. Although politicians have thus far been the primary beneficiaries of the policy[2], the political benefits of pursuing prohibition are now waning and the political costs of its continuation are becoming unsustainable. The intellectual and political consensus supporting a 'War on Drugs' is crumbling rapidly, and calls for 'more of the same', or ever tougher enforcement responses, no longer go unchallenged. Since the 1990s, a vigorous network of domestic and international NGOs have been making the case for substantive pragmatic reform to drug policy and law[3].

> "Never have so many dangerous drugs been seized by police and Customs. But never have so many drugs been taken nor has so much crime been caused by them. However much is done to stop the threat, the drugs industry – and it is an industry – is several jumps ahead. It is obvious that something new needs to be tried."
>
> DAILY MIRROR LEADER EDITORIAL – 25.06.03

However, although the failure of the current policy is now widely accepted, even within government, there is less consensus on 'so, where now?'. Those in a state of denial over the failure of the drug war typically argue that policy can be tweaked within the prohibitionist framework to make it more effective. This usually means directing more resources into treatment and harm reduction, and perhaps being more tolerant of low level drug users. There is considerable room for manoeuvre within UK and international law[4] for policies that could improve the current situation and indeed many such changes are already underway. In recent years we have seen cannabis reclassification, the expansion of heroin and methadone prescribing, harm reduction programs such as the needle exchanges and 'injecting kits', and increased investment in drug treatment.

Internationally, reforms have gone much further. A number of countries have progressed to de facto decriminalision of personal possession of all drugs, including Russia, Portugal, Spain, Switzerland and Holland. Harm reduction measures have been widely adopted, including maintenance prescribing of heroin (and increasingly of stimulants), supervised drug consumption rooms, and even tolerance of low level sales of some drugs, such as the cannabis 'coffee shop' system in Holland.

The problem is that, for the most part, these reforms are merely reducing harms created by illegal markets and harshly enforced prohibition in the first place. They never address its fundamental problems: the creation of crime and illegal markets and the injustice of criminalising drug users. Tinkering with domestic policy under strict international prohibition is not a long term solution. It is an attempt to minimise harms within a legal framework that maximises them, and thus its successes will always be marginal ones.

By contrast, the truth that underlies the drug reform movement - that a punitive enforcement approach is actively counter-productive – is far harder to address directly. This prevents it being followed to its obvious logical conclusion: decriminalising consenting adult drug use and moving towards the legal regulation and control of some or all drug production and supply

Yet this last taboo is now also crumbling, as Transform's collection of quotes from supporters of reform (see box) so resoundingly demonstrates. The Transform quote archive also reveals that there have been strong arguments in favour of drug law reform in media as diverse as the Mirror, the Sun, the Daily Mail, the Telegraph, The Times, the Economist, the New Statesman and many others besides. You really do not have to wait for the reform position to gain mainstream traction – it already has .

Whilst it remains important to support and encourage the process of incremental change away from harshly enforced prohibition towards a new evidence-based public health approach, there are already many groups dedicated to doing this and much change is already happening in this direction. The specific task of Transform and the movement for longer term reform is to make the case and campaign for a repeal of the absolute drug prohibition currently enshrined in domestic and international law. It is only this fundamental step that will make it possible to end the criminal free-for-all of the illegal drugs market by replacing it with appropriately regulated drug production and supply. That is what will lead to a real transformation of society, both for those who use drugs and those who don't; and that is what this guide is all about.

STEVE ROLLES
LONDON 2007

"IF GOVERNMENT-CONTROLLED DRUGS WERE CHEAPLY AVAILABLE, MIGHT IT NOT CUT THROUGH THIS HIDEOUS VICIOUS CIRCLE? USERS WOULDN'T NEED TO FUND THEIR HABIT BY MAKING OUR LIVES HELL. DEALERS, MEANWHILE, WOULD FIND NOBODY TO BUY THEIR OVERPRICED, ADULTERATED WARES. WE COULD SPEND EVERY PENNY SAVED FROM ENFORCEMENT AND IMPRISONMENT AND DRUG-RELATED CRIME ON TREATMENT, PREVENTION AND EDUCATING PEOPLE NOT TO TAKE THE STUPID THINGS IN THE FIRST PLACE"

THE SUN: 'WHY NOT LEGALISE DRUGS...IT WORKED FINE THE LAST TIME' 12.11.05

WHO SUPPORTS REFORM?

Advocates of drug policy and law reform now encompass an astonishingly broad spectrum of political thought, including prominent thinkers from all major political parties, numerous world leaders, Nobel laureates, senior police, ex-ministers, religious leaders, academics, authors, artists and intellectuals. Quotes from many of these individuals and agencies are provided throughout this document, and Transform has also produced a unique indexed archive of referenced quotes which can be viewed online here: www.tdpf.org.uk/MediaNews_Reform_supporters. This extensive and often surprising collection of quotes emphasises how holding a progressive position on drug policy is no longer an extreme position, but a legitimate, even mainstream view. If anything, it is the shrill advocates of prohibition who are increasingly marginalised as irrational extremists and ideologues.

1. FAULTLINES IN THE DRUG POLICY DEBATE: UNDERSTANDING THE DIFFERENT MINDSETS

THIS CHAPTER CONSIDERS THE KEY FAULT LINES IN THE DRUG DEBATE: ON THE ONE SIDE THE IDEOLOGICAL POSITIONS UNDERLYING PROHIBITION, AND ON THE OTHER THE RATIONAL ARGUMENTS FOR REFORM. IN DOING SO IT AIMS TO PROVIDE THE FRAMEWORK FOR THE ANALYSIS AND DEBATING TECHNIQUES THAT FORM THE MAIN BODY OF THIS GUIDE.

FIRSTLY, WHAT IS PROHIBITION?

Any activity or product can in theory be prohibited by law. Specifically, drug prohibition is a globalised legal system (under the UN drug treaties 1961, 1971, and 1988, signed into the domestic law of over 150 states including the UK) that mandates criminal sanctions for the production, supply and possession/use of certain psychoactive drugs, although the sanctions/penalties for different offences vary widely between countries.

The stated aim of prohibition is to reduce the production, supply and use of the specified drugs, and ultimately to create a 'drug-free society'. The policy of drug prohibition has often been referred to as the 'War on Drugs', one of many military metaphors originally employed by US governments in the 1970s.

The term 'prohibition' is used in the UK's 2002 updated National Drug Strategy, and by Government ministers and Home Office officials in reference to current drug policy. The 1998 United Nations Drug Control Programme ten year strategy, to which the UK is a signatory, has the slogan: "A Drug Free World: We Can Do It!" and established as its objective the eradication (or significant reduction) of illicit opium, coca and cannabis production worldwide by 2008.

The public understanding of the word 'prohibition' (often written with a capital P) derives from the alcohol prohibition era from 1920 to 1932 in the US, popularised by gangster films about characters such as Al Capone. For this reason it may be useful to clarify early on that you are talking about 'contemporary' or 'modern drug prohibition', or the 'current prohibition of certain drugs'. Alcohol prohibition was a thirteen year experiment that failed in dramatic style. It was eventually repealed, with alcohol brought back within a legal regulatory framework.

Using the term 'prohibition' to describe current drug policy can be a useful way of highlighting the similarity between the problems of modern drug prohibition and historical alcohol prohibition - widely understood to have been repealed because it was expensive, counterproductive and created significant health and crime harms. Today's drug problems closely mirror those in the USA in 1930, except that they now encompass many more drugs, and a vastly enlarged and global illegal market. (see: FAQ on prohibtion[5], and: History of prohibition timeline[1])

It is important to make a distinction between drug prohibition as described here - which puts an absolute prohibition on the production, supply and use of certain substances, and regulated drug markets (e.g. alcohol) under which some activities are legal and some remain prohibited (eg. sales to minors, purchase outside of licensed premises). Prohibition is an absolutist position, whereas its repeal opens the door for a wide variety of possible regulatory options (see chapter 4 - 'Making the case for regulated markets' for more discussion on this)

SUMMARY TABLE OF KEY FAULT LINES IN THE DEBATE BETWEEN PROHIBITIONIST AND REFORM POSITIONS

Those who support the prohibition of drugs tend to share a set of underlying assumptions about why these drugs are prohibited, and why it is important that they should remain so. Those who advocate reform of drug policy tend to do so on the basis of a different set of assumptions. The table below sets out the assumptions that typically lie behind these two polarised positions.

STATUS QUO POSITION*	REFORM POSITION
Illegal drug use must be eradicated	People have always used drugs, and always will
Any use of illegal drugs is problematic	Most illegal drug use is non-problematic. Many of the health harms associated with illegal drug use are caused by their illegality
Problematic drug use is caused by using drugs	Problematic drug use is primarily a symptom of underlying personal or social problems. Drugs can exacerbate underlying problems
Drugs make people lose control and behave dangerously	People often take drugs partly to lose control (but it can get out of control)
Legalisation and regulation is a step into the unknown	We have centuries of experience in legally regulating thousands of different drugs
Drug law reform is being forced through by the 'liberal elite'	Drug law reform is supported by individuals from across the social and political spectrum
Prohibition protects the health of individuals	Prohibition creates new public health problems and maximises harms associated with illegal drug use
Prohibition sends an important message about avoiding drugs and their dangers	The criminal justice system should not be used to send public health messages
Prohibition reduces the prevalence of use, and limits experimentation	Prevalence of use has risen dramatically under prohibition. Enforcement activity is, at best, a marginal influence on levels of use which rise and fall largely independently of policy and law

STATUS QUO POSITION	REFORM POSITION
Harm reduction encourages drug use	Harm reduction saves lives. Trying to discourage drug use by maximising harm is unethical and ineffective.
Reduced prevalence is the most important indicator of policy success	Reduced harm is the most important indicator of policy success
Increased availability leads to increased drug use and hence to increased problematic use. Prohibition creates a barrier against temptation and chaos	Increased availability may increase use, but well regulated availability will certainly reduce harm. Prohibition leads many into temptation and is creating criminal chaos
Calling for legalisation and regulation brings the law into disrepute	Counterproductive enforcement brings the law into disrepute
Prohibition is based on a strong moral position that drugs are unacceptable	The policy that is most effective at reducing harm and maximising well being is the moral position
A strong ideological stand is more important than effectiveness	Measurable effectiveness is more important than ideology
Human rights issues of users can be ignored	Human rights issues of users and the wider community are paramount
Drugs are dangerous and should be prohibited	Drugs are dangerous and should be appropriately controlled and regulated
Prohibition controls drug use and drug markets	Prohibition abdicates control of illegal drug production and supply to the criminal networks and unregulated dealers
Ending prohibition would automatically hand control of the trade to multinational corporations (who would aggressively market drugs)	Ending prohibition allows for various models of control and regulation and takes the market away from criminals (who already aggressively market drugs)
The health, social and financial costs of prohibition are a price worth paying	Prohibition is hugely costly and counterproductive on most indicators
Underlying causes of problematic use can be addressed within a prohibitionist framework	Prohibition causes and exacerbates many problems associated with illegal drug use, and is an obstacle to addressing underlying causes
We must not 'give up' the fight against illegal drugs	Drug policies should be adapted in response to evidence of effectiveness
Prohibition is 'tough on drugs'	Prohibition creates a 'gangster's charter'
Producer countries are willfully ignoring global prohibition	Producer countries are unintentionally pushed into illegal production by the economics of illegal drug markets under global prohibition

* Inevitably these are generalisations, and not necessarily the precise policy positions of any individual

DIFFERENT AUDIENCES IN THE DEBATE

These starkly opposed assumptions mean that the drugs debate is often conducted between groups of people who see the issues around drugs and their control very differently. You will encounter a range of different audiences in the political, media, NGO or public arenas, who have a range of different views on drug policy and policy reform. It is important to adapt your approach accordingly. The positions that you will find yourself arguing against can be roughly categorised as follows:

- EVANGELICAL PROHIBITIONISTS

These tend to be people directly involved in drug enforcement; those who have a strong faith position (where drug use often equates to 'sin'); or, occasionally those who have had bad personal experiences with illegal drugs. (Note: none of these backgrounds preclude supporting reform – see: Transform's archive of high profile supporters of reform). Always remember and respect the fact that these views are usually sincere and well-intentioned - they may have witnessed real drug related harm, are fearful it will get worse and passionately want to prevent it. To them drugs are a Pandora's Box, and prohibition – the law - is keeping the lid on it. They genuinely believe that 'legalisation' (as they perceive it) would pry open the box, cost lives and make the world a worse place. As such, they see themselves as prohibition's principled guardians and advocates of law reform as their natural enemies.

Such views may be so deeply entrenched that there is little point trying to turn them round - it can be like arguing Darwinism with committed creationists. Sometimes the best you can achieve with such individuals or audiences is to use any public forum as an opportunity to put your views across, contrasting your rational reform position with the ideological prohibitionist one – and let the audience make their own minds up. That said, in Transform's experience many of the least likely people, including some of our seemingly most implacable opponents, have in time been won over. Never give up hope, but be ready to cut your losses.

- KNEE-JERK PROHIBITIONISTS

'Knee-jerk' isn't meant here in any rude way, maybe 'prohibitionists by default' would be a good alternative term. These are people, probably constituting the bulk of your audience, who default to supporting some or most of the prohibitionist positions outlined above on the basis of exposure to one sided discourse and debate over a number of years. It is important to remember that, superficially at least, drug war rhetoric is very appealing, especially when unchallenged in mainstream debate by any coherent alternative. This audience's position is based on ignorance of the reform analysis, rather than entrenched ideology, and is fertile ground for informing and changing perceptions. The shifting public opinion on cannabis reform (15% supporting decriminalisation/legalisation in the mid 80s, to over 50% today[7]) provides strong evidence of how exposure to informed debate on this issue invariably pushes people in the direction of supporting reform.

- UNCONVINCED REFORMERS

This audience is your most receptive target. These are people who understand the failings of the current system and instinctively know that 'something needs to be done', but they are unclear what that might be. In the absence of a clear argument being made for moves towards legal regulation they will generally not feel inclined to challenge reforms being put forward by government, such as increased coerced treatment or harsh criminal justice crackdowns and 'get tough' initiatives. Their views on legal regulation may be clouded by misunderstandings about 'legalisation' (see: 'from 'legalisation' to 'regulation' p.33), put forward by cannabis evangelists or extreme libertarians. When they are presented with a coherent set of policy alternatives this group will usually be happy to support them.

- PROHIBITIONIST POLITICIANS

There is a fourth audience – the prohibitionist politicians, potentially the most important audience of all but often the most unequivocal and effective opponents of reform. As discussed earlier (see foreword) the drug policy debate operates at an entirely different level to the rational / scientific one. It is important to bear in mind that many politicians hold a hard-line prohibitionist position for self-interested and career reasons – they are self-appointed 'drug warriors'. Usually they are senior parliamentarians (ministers and their shadows), their spokespeople and the civil servants who back them up. They will trot out a 'tough on drugs' party line and back it up with a well-practiced repertoire of moral outrage or evasion, regardless of their personal views. They are the nearest thing you will encounter to a mortal enemy in this debate: they know their case is indefensible but argue it anyway. They are treating an important debate with disdain and in doing so are perpetuating a system they know to be harmful. No amount of brilliant argument will sway them because they are not interested in genuine intellectual debate or new ideas. If you have thoughts on how to influence this group please get in touch with us.

THE FAULT LINES WITHIN CURRENT DRUG POLICY

As a way of demonstrating the fault lines in the drug debate, consider the two pieces of text juxtaposed overleaf. On the left is the introduction to the Alcohol Harm Reduction Strategy by the Prime Minister Tony Blair, published in March 2004 . In many respects it reflects the reformer's perspective on the drug debate fault lines described above: an acceptance of the reality of drug use (in this case alcohol) in the UK and a rational strategy to minimise alcohol related harm, both to consumers and to wider society, through a series of pragmatic regulatory responses based on evidence of effectiveness. On the right is the identical text with one minor editorial change made by Transform: the word 'alcohol' has been changed to 'drugs', and the word 'drinking' has been changed to 'drug use'. This juxtaposition demonstrates that the fault lines in this debate, once the 'hot button' issue of drugs is removed, are by no means as polarised as they appear. The exact same fault lines actually exist within current drug policy.

Bizarrely, the Government is simultaneously running, on the one hand, a policy on legal drugs based on using public health and evidence led regulation to minimise harm, and on the other hand a policy on illegal drugs that ignores evidence of effectiveness and uses the criminal justice system to enforce a dogmatic moral view.

Transform have read out the revised version of the text below (right) in debates to great effect. It really forces people to think (and, whilst not meant as a joke, sometimes gets a few laughs).

WHY THIS...BUT NOT THIS?

WHY THIS ...

Millions of us enjoy drinking alcohol with few, if any, ill effects. Indeed moderate drinking can bring some health benefits. But, increasingly, alcohol misuse by a small minority is causing two major, and largely distinct, problems: on the one hand crime and anti-social behaviour in town and city centres, and on the other harm to health as a result of binge- and chronic drinking.

The Strategy Unit's analysis last year showed that alcohol - related harm is costing around £20bn a year , and that some of the harms associated with alcohol are getting worse.

This is why the Government has been looking at how best to tackle the problems of alcohol misuse. The aim has been to target alcohol-related harm and its causes without interfering with the pleasure enjoyed by the millions of people who drink responsibly.

This report sets out the way forward. Alongside the interim report published last year it describes in detail the current patterns of drinking – and the specific harms associated with alcohol . And it clearly shows that the best way to minimise the harms is through partnership between government, local authorities, police, industry and the public themselves.

... BUT NOT THIS?

Millions of us enjoy drug use with few, if any, ill effects. Indeed moderate drug use can bring some health benefits. But, increasingly, drug misuse by a small minority is causing two major, and largely distinct, problems: on the one hand crime and anti-social behaviour in town and city centres, and on the other harm to health as a result of binge- and chronic drug use .

The Strategy Unit's analysis last year showed that drug-related harm is costing around £20bn a year, and that some of the harms associated with drugs are getting worse.

This is why the Government has been looking at how best to tackle the problems of drug misuse. The aim has been to target drug-related harm and its causes without interfering with the pleasure enjoyed by the millions of people who use drugs responsibly.

This report sets out the way forward. Alongside the interim report published last year it describes in detail the current patterns of drug use – and the specific harms associated with drugs . And it clearly shows that the best way to minimise the harms is through partnership between government, local authorities, police, industry and the public themselves.

WHY THIS ...

For government, the priority is to work with the police and local authorities so that existing laws to reduce alcohol-related crime and disorder are properly enforced, including powers to shut down any premises where there is a serious problem of disorder arising from it. Treatment services need to be able to meet demand. And the public needs access to clear information setting out the full and serious effects of heavy drinking.

For the drinks industry, the priority is to end irresponsible promotions and advertising; to better ensure the safety of their staff and customers; and to limit the nuisance caused to local communities.

Ultimately, however, it is vital that individuals can make informed and responsible decisions about their own levels of alcohol consumption. Everyone needs to be able to balance their right to enjoy a drink with the potential risks to their own – and others' – health and wellbeing. Young people in particular need to better understand the risks involved in harmful patterns of drinking.

I strongly welcome this report and the Government has accepted all its conclusions. These will now be implemented as government policy and will, in time, bring benefits to us all in the form of a healthier and happier relationship with alcohol.

Tony Blair

Foreword to the Alcohol Harm Reduction Strategy for England
Cabinet Office
Prime Minister's Strategy Unit, March 2004

... BUT NOT THIS?

For government, the priority is to work with the police and local authorities so that existing laws to reduce drug-related crime and disorder are properly enforced, including powers to shut down any premises where there is a serious problem of disorder arising from it. Treatment services need to be able to meet demand. And the public needs access to clear information setting out the full and serious effects of heavy drug use.

For the drugs industry, the priority is to end irresponsible promotions and advertising; to better ensure the safety of their staff and customers; and to limit the nuisance caused to local communities.

Ultimately, however, it is vital that individuals can make informed and responsible decisions about their own levels of drug consumption. Everyone needs to be able to balance their right to enjoy using drugs with the potential risks to their own – and others' – health and wellbeing. Young people in particular need to better understand the risks involved in harmful patterns of drug use.

I strongly welcome this report and the Government has accepted all its conclusions. These will now be implemented as government policy and will, in time, bring benefits to us all in the form of a healthier and happier relationship with drugs.

Tony Blair

Foreword to the Drug Harm Reduction Strategy for England
Cabinet Office (with edits by Transform)
Prime Minister's Strategy Unit, March 2004

2. FINDING COMMON GROUND – BRINGING THE TWO SIDES TOGETHER

THE FAULT LINES OUTLINED ABOVE HAVE, IN TRANSFORM'S EXPERIENCE, HELD BACK THE DRUG POLICY DEBATE FOR MANY YEARS. TOO OFTEN, PARTICULARLY IN THE MEDIA, COMPLEX ISSUES ARE REDUCED TO A KNOCKABOUT BETWEEN THE HARD-LINE PROHIBITIONIST 'DRUG WARRIORS' ON ONE SIDE AND THE 'LIBERAL' REFORMERS OR 'LEGALISERS' ON THE OTHER.

"WE CAN AGREE ABOUT MANY THINGS. ALL DRUGS ARE BAD AND WE OUGHT TO REDUCE THEM. THE ONE WAY THAT ONE DOES NOT DEAL WITH SOMETHING THAT IS DANGEROUS AND BAD IS TO HAND IT LOCK STOCK AND BARREL TO ORGANISED CRIME. THAT IS WHAT THE MISUSE OF DRUGS ACT 1971 DOES. THE PROBLEM IS NOT PROHIBITION, THE PROBLEM IS THE FAILURE OF PROHIBITION. THE ONLY WAY THAT ONE CAN CONTROL A DANGEROUS COMMODITY OR ANY COMMODITY IS TO BRING IT WITHIN THE LAW. WE NEED TO REPEAL THE MISUSE OF DRUGS ACT 1971 AND REPLACE IT WITH A BETTER AND MORE APPROPRIATE TOOL THAT ALLOWS US TO CONTROL THE MARKET IN THOSE INCREDIBLY DANGEROUS COMMODITIES. AT THAT STAGE WE CAN REMOVE THE PROFIT, REMOVE THE CRIME AND DEVOTE ALL OF OUR RESOURCES AND ENERGIES TO PROVIDING BETTER TREATMENT AND REAL PREVENTION. AT THE MOMENT WE ARE NOT DOING THAT, AND WE SHALL NOT IF THE GOVERNMENT CONTINUE DOWN THEIR PRESENT PATH."

LORD MANCROFT, CONSERVATIVE PEER

HANSARD, HOUSE OF LORDS DEBATE 11.06.03

Participants on both sides of the fault line have often been guilty of misunderstanding and misrepresenting each others' positions, rarely showing any willingness to listen or give ground. The result is a repetitive debate that invariably creates more heat than light and never progresses beyond conflict or stalemate. This polarisation (often driven by the media's desire to present a clash between strongly contrasting views) is a barrier to reform, and must be overcome before real change can take place. Progress requires the two apparently irreconcilable sides of this debate to find some common ground and adopt a new language that will enable meaningful dialogue. This chapter aims to show how to find common ground in the debate about the aims and principles of an effective drugs policy.

In reality the policy debate is nowhere near as black and white as the media debate portrays it to be. It is not a battle between 'pro' and 'anti' drug campaigners, left and right, liberals and conservatives, or any other stark binary choice. It needs to become a rational, intelligent and sophisticated debate over the range of policy alternatives for addressing the issues of drugs in society.

It is important, therefore, should you be engaging in this debate in the media or any public forum, not to let yourself be pushed in the direction of a polarised emotive debate merely for sake of audience entertainment. Whilst there does exist a broad spectrum of views (from extreme authoritarian prohibition to extreme free

THE PARADOX OF PROHIBITION *

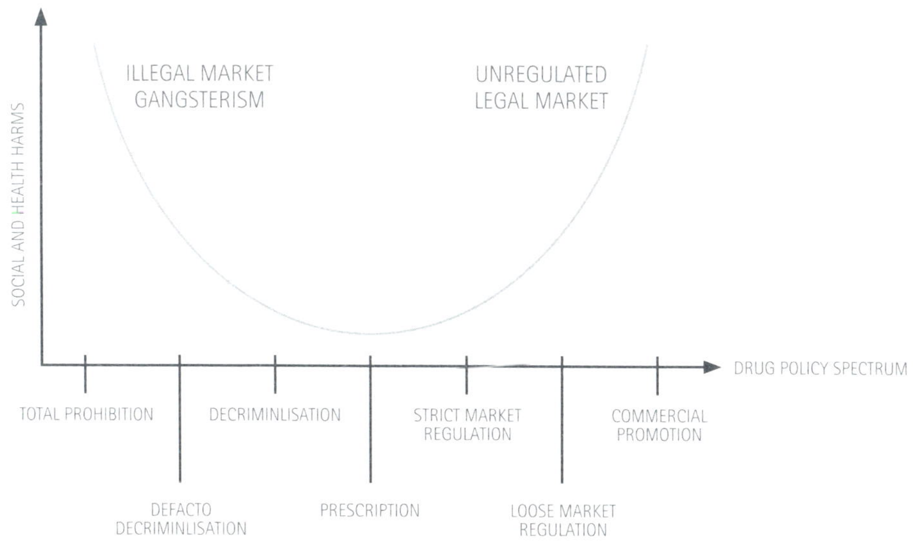

* THANKS TO JOHN MARKS AND MARK HADEN

market legalisation) almost everybody, including Transform, lies somewhere between the two, usually nearer the middle - and each other - than at either extreme.

Transform advocates the regulated central point on this graphic model – on the basis that this is the one that causes the least harm. This guide is about making the case for that position

It is important to note that the different sides of this debate do not equate easily to broader political or ideological fault lines. The status quo / reform fault line is not simply the authoritarian / libertarian divide, nor the right-wing / left-wing divide, nor the socially conservative / socially liberal divide. This is a simplistic analysis, shaped largely by the media's need for dialectical drama.

Drug policy reform is supported by prominent thinkers and intellectuals from across the political spectrum, from Noam Chomsky to Milton Friedman, from members of all major parties in the UK and in the US, and from countries with a wide range of social, economic, political and cultural landscapes (again, see the Transform archive of supporters of reform[6]). Some advocates of reform envisage replacing prohibition with a libertarian regime, others with draconian forms of social control. The reform argument itself is non partisan – it is simply a pragmatic position led by evidence of effectiveness and public health / harm reduction principles. Calling for legally regulated drug markets is actually the rational and moderate position between the ideological poles of absolute prohibition and free market libertarianism.

The suggestion that the drug law reform movement intends to 'liberalise' or 'relax' the drug laws is a common misconception that must be challenged. Advocates of law reform want more control and regulation of drug markets, not less. We are specifically calling for more and better regulation, and are specifically critical of the deregulation and lack of control that prohibition creates.

AGREEING ON THE PRINCIPLES UNDERLYING DRUG POLICY

The first step towards establishing useful common ground is to point out that there are aims of drug policy, and principles under which it should operate, that everyone in this debate can agree on. The principles and aims listed below will not meet with substantial disagreement (with some specific exceptions – see notes) and as such can successfully provide the starting point for more constructive debate between the advocates of alternative policy positions.

Establishing agreement on these fundamentals will allow you to maintain some control over the debate, defuse the anticipated tensions, appeal to the shared concerns of all participants, and create some breathing room in which a meaningful discussion can take place. From this point the debate can develop in a more constructive and rational way towards asking which policy alternatives are likely to bring about these policy aims we all seek.

A table appended at the end of the guide (p.63) uses these common ground principles and aims as the basis for a more detailed point by point critique of prohibition, and case for reform.

- ALL DRUGS ARE POTENTIALLY DANGEROUS, AND ALL DRUG USE IS INTRINSICALLY RISKY

Making this point clear early on immediately establishes distance between you and any

MEDIA PITFALLS

Where possible, attempt to engage in forums where more detailed analysis is possible – whether this be a decent length for an article or a reasonable time to discuss issues in broadcast media or public debate. There is a real problem trying to present often complex and nuanced analysis in the media which puts huge emphasis on concision – often only a couple of sentences in print or 30 seconds or less in broadcast. For many people the idea of legalising and regulating drugs is, initially at least, quite shocking. You need a reasonable amount of time to clarify what you are calling for, make your case, and back it up with facts and argument.

If you are pushed for time/space then you will need to work extra hard at making what you say as clear as possible – potentially boiling your points down to short 'soundbites', however unsatisfactory this may be. Throughout this guide we have included useful examples in the form of quotations from the great and good. Take a lead from these and if necessary work out your own in advance. Everyone in policy debate is playing the same game – it's a fact of life

preconceptions about the law reform position being 'pro-drug' (a meaningless term anyway) or somehow 'defending' drugs or suggesting they are safe or cool. It also takes the sting out of many anti-regulation/legalisation arguments that revolve around shock/horror facts and anecdotes about how dangerous drug use is. As we will see later, the fact that drugs are potentially dangerous is at the core of the argument for their effective regulation.

• DRUG POLICY SHOULD BE BASED ON EVIDENCE OF EFFECTIVENESS

This is the standard pragmatist's argument, usefully engaging with the policy maker's language and concern with 'what works?'. It is a key point to emphasise, firstly because no-one can seriously make a rational argument against it (that we either shouldn't consider the evidence or that policy should be based on evidence of ineffectiveness), and secondly because it draws the debate away from the ideological fault lines, and towards the reality of prohibition's failure. Emphasising evidence of effectiveness is a key part of re-conceptualising the debate as a rational/scientific one rather than a moral/ideological one.

• DRUG POLICY SHOULD OFFER GOOD VALUE FOR MONEY

This is essentially the same as the above principle that drug policy should be based on evidence of effectiveness, but has a more direct appeal to people's pockets: both policy makers who have to decide how to allocate limited budgets, and the wider public who, as tax payers, are the ones funding drug prohibition in the first instance. Emphasising this principle is another useful way of focusing debate on policy outcomes (rather than processes) and evidence of effectiveness.

Because enforcement-led policy offers stunningly poor value for money - it is hugely expensive and creates further costs to society - economics is very fertile territory for arguing the reform position.

- POLICY SHOULD BE BASED ON REALITY AND ADAPT TO CHANGING CIRCUMSTANCES

This principle also follows from broader pragmatic argument, but is worth spelling out. What seems obvious for all policy - that it should be based on reality - is less clear for the prohibitionist paradigm, the goals of which remain intimately entwined with a mission to promote abstinence and regulate pleasure. Given society's deep-rooted dependencies on alcohol, tobacco and prescription drugs (not to mention numerous other 'vices' and 'sinful' pleasures) the idea that we can become free of precisely those drugs whose effects are pleasurable becomes an absurdity. But prohibition and its legal structures remain rooted in these puritanical principles, despite the fact that the social landscape has changed beyond recognition in the 50 years or so since the UN drug conventions were drafted. Furthermore, these conventions were drafted, largely at the behest of the US, to deal with a marginal drug problem largely confined to ethnic minorities and career criminals, not the huge swathes of the population who use illicit drugs today.

- DRUG POLICY IS PRIMARILY A PUBLIC HEALTH ISSUE

This is a more contentious point to make and needs further careful development (see chapter 4, p.35). However, if you do succeed in moving the debate towards your position that drugs are primarily a public health issue, the prohibitionists are obliged to argue why it shouldn't be - or, more specifically, why certain drugs should be dealt with as a public health issue (e.g. alcohol) and others primarily as criminal activity (see 'the fault lines within existing policy' p15).

- POLICY SHOULD SEEK TO REDUCE DRUG RELATED HARM

Again this may prove more contentious. Transform maintain that the overarching aim of drug policy should be to minimise harm and maximise well-being. Within this overarching objective we can identify a number of specific aims to reduce harms related to drug production, supply and use, with success measured against relevant indicators (including reduction in demand/use). Prohibitionists traditionally maintain that the aim of policy is to reduce the use of drugs and ultimately to achieve a drug free society. This aim sometimes has the feel of religious dogma - a commandment to which all policy aims must remain loyal, if the promised land of the drug-free world is to be attained[9].

It is important to point out that some 'drug related harms' are associated with drug use and misuse itself, while others are specifically created or exacerbated by the enforcement of prohibitionist policy and law (e.g. reusing dirty needles, crime to support an illegal drug habit). Consequently, reducing specific prohibition-related harms feature within the aims of drug policy reform, but become a thing of the past under a legally regulated regime. As an analogy, reducing car exhaust emissions would no longer be an aim of transport policy if everyone was driving solar-powered electric cars.

As you engage in the debate try to keep this distinction in mind, making it clear that there is a difference between the aims of drug policy reform, (essentially to remove the harms created by prohibition: see appendix p.63), and the aims of drug policy itself (to maximise well-being and minimise health and social harms related to drug use and misuse). This also helps to highlight how, when prohibition is replaced, we will be in a far better position to address the underlying social ills that fuel most problematic drug use.

AIMS OF DRUG POLICY

As developed by Transform, the core aims of drug policy, which can only be properly addressed once the current prohibition of drugs is dismantled, are:

- TO MINIMISE THE PREVALENCE OF PROBLEMATIC DRUG USE AND RELATED HEALTH HARMS, INCLUDING DRUG RELATED DEATH.

Although this sounds uncontroversial, it actually challenges a central tenet of current drug policy: that any illicit drug use is unacceptable / illegal, and / or that non-problematic drug use does not exist. However, this assertion ignores the reality that problematic drug users, defined by the need for social or criminal justice intervention, are in reality only a small fraction of the drug-using population. Transform argues that non-problematic use should not be the primary concern of Government, beyond efforts to prevent progression into problematic use, which can be supported on public health grounds if there is evidence that they are effective.

- TO MINIMISE DISORDER, VIOLENCE AND SOCIAL NUISANCE RELATED TO DRUG USE.

- TO MINIMISE CRIMINAL ACTIVITY ASSOCIATED WITH THE PRODUCTION AND SUPPLY OF DRUGS

These two aims are linked; however, there is a clear distinction between public order problems caused by intoxication (overwhelmingly by alcohol) and the far more significant problems caused by illegal markets.

- TO MINIMISE DRUG-RELATED HARM TO VULNERABLE GROUPS, YOUNG PEOPLE AND FAMILIES

Whilst the ethics of dictating personal behaviour to adults is a tricky area, for non-adults there are clear arguments for programmes to prevent early drug use as a public health initiative and as part of a wider harm reduction approach.

- TO ENSURE ADEQUATE PROVISION OF SUPPORT AND DRUG TREATMENT FOR PEOPLE SEEKING HELP

Some may argue that drug users don't deserve care or should not be allowed to receive the benefit of non-drug-using taxpayers' money. It's a potentially thorny area (as recent debates on restricting certain treatments/procedures to alcoholics/smokers have shown). It can be avoided by highlighting the positive cost-benefit analysis of treatment versus continuation of chaotic drug use.

The appendix (p.63) presents a summary table, using the principles and aims outlined above, to highlight the problems with prohibition and the benefits of legal regulation.

> **"PROHIBITION DOESN'T WORK, AS THE US FOUND OUT MANY YEARS AGO."**
>
> **JOHN REID MP, HOME SECRETARY**
> **DISCUSSING TOBACCO POLICY, JEREMY VINE PROGRAMME, BBC RADIO 2, 11.11.04**

3. CRITIQUING THE FAILINGS OF CURRENT POLICY

ONCE SOME COMMON GROUND HAS BEEN ESTABLISHED ON THE AIMS AND PRINCIPLES UNDERLYING DRUG POLICY, THE NEXT LOGICAL STEP IS TO CRITIQUE PROHIBITION BASED ON THESE AGREED AIMS AND PRINCIPLES. GENERALLY SPEAKING, THIS IS NOT ESPECIALLY DIFFICULT, AS PROHIBITION HAS FAILED ON ALMOST EVERY INDICATOR IMAGINABLE. THE KEY HERE, GIVEN THAT YOU ARE BEING LISTENED TO IN THE FIRST PLACE, IS SIMPLY TO MAKE SURE YOU HAVE THE BASIC FACTS AND ANALYSIS AT YOUR FINGER TIPS.

BEAR IN MIND, HOWEVER, THAT NO POLICY WHICH HAS BEEN SUCH A SPECTACULAR AND CONSISTENT FAILURE COULD HAVE BEEN SUSTAINED FOR SO LONG WITHOUT A MONUMENTAL PROPAGANDA EFFORT TO PROP IT UP. AS YOU CRITIQUE PROHIBITION YOU WILL NEED TO BE AWARE OF THE FOREST OF MISINFORMATION, MYTH, AND STATISTICAL CHICANERY THAT DEFENDS IT, SO THAT YOU CAN CUT THROUGH IT WHEN NECESSARY.

"ON ISSUES LIKE SMOKING, DRINKING AND GAMBLING, GOVERNMENT HAS THREE BASIC CHOICES: WE CAN PROHIBIT, REGULATE OR LEAVE IT TO THE MARKET. PROHIBITION DOES NOT WORK - IT DRIVES THE ACTIVITY UNDERGROUND .... ONLY IDEOLOGICAL EXTREMISTS FAVOUR A FREE-FOR-ALL WHERE ONLY THE LAWS OF THE MARKET HOLD SWAY. SO THE THIRD OPTION IS REGULATION...'BETTER REGULATION' HAS TO MEAN GOVERNMENT ENGAGING PEOPLE IN THE DECISIONS THAT AFFECT THEIR LIVES AND DOING SO IN NEW AND BETTER WAYS".

TESSA JOWELL MP, MINISTER OF CULTURE
'GROWN UP POLITICS FOR AN ADULT WORLD' THE GUARDIAN 21.11.04

CHALLENGING PROHIBITIONIST MYTHS AND MISINFORMATION

There are numerous myths perpetuated by the defenders of current drug policy, most of them aimed at supporting the case that prohibition is effective. Quite simply, it isn't, as even a cursory examination of the facts reveals.

Prohibition was intended to eliminate drugs from the world and has achieved the exact opposite. On a consistent basis, over more than two generations, drug production has risen, drug consumption has risen, drug availability has risen (whilst prices have fallen), and drug related health problems have risen. Crucially, in addition, prohibition has directly created a raft of new problems associated with criminal markets locally and narco-states globally. Once an illegal market has become established, prohibition has not worked anywhere, ever. Moreover it has been universally and quite spectacularly counterproductive on all meaningful indicators.

The myth of prohibition's effectiveness is constructed from a series of assertions that can very easily be demolished:

1. PROHIBITION REDUCES AVAILABILITY

This is perhaps the most easily-refuted claim made for prohibition – so much so that you rarely hear it anymore. Nevertheless, the goal of reducing the availability of drugs remains a key pillar of the UK national drug strategy, and indeed of the entire UN international drug control apparatus. Reducing availability remains the sole aim of supply-side enforcement at the international, domestic and local levels, absorbing billions of government spending each year[10].

The simplistic rationale for this strategy is that if drug supply can be stopped then no one will take drugs and the drug problem will disappear. However, drug markets are demand-driven, and supplying them is a staggeringly lucrative business. Consistently, over several generations, and in countries across the world, there has been a clear trend of drug supply and use steadily increasing. Drugs are cheaper and more available today than at any time previously, something that even official analysis from the Home Office, the ACMD[11], and even Tony Blair's own confidential report produced for him by his Number 10 Strategy Unit[12] does not dispute. Never let anyone claim that supply side enforcement is effective without a very robust challenge – the evidence against this assertion is clear, overwhelming and acknowledged by all credible sources, official and independent.

2. PROHIBITION REDUCES USE / IS AN EFFECTIVE DETERRENT

This myth is entwined within the previous one, that prohibition reduces drug availability; but it also depends on the concept of using enforcement to 'send out the right message' on drugs, namely that they are harmful to health and you shouldn't take them. The concept of criminal law as a deterrent to drug use is absolutely central to the entire prohibitionist paradigm, and yet the assumption has little or no evidential foundation. This is a point that you can raise with great confidence whenever the deterrent issue arises:

- Drug use has risen faster under prohibition than at any time in human history.

- International comparisons show no correlation between the harshness of enforcement

"WESTERN GOVERNMENTS ... WILL LOSE THE WAR AGAINST DEALERS UNLESS EFFORTS ARE SWITCHED TO PREVENTION AND THERAPY... ALL PENALTIES FOR DRUG USERS SHOULD BE DROPPED ... MAKING DRUG ABUSE A CRIME IS USELESS AND EVEN DANGEROUS ... EVERY YEAR WE SEIZE MORE AND MORE DRUGS AND ARREST MORE AND MORE DEALERS BUT AT THE SAME TIME THE QUANTITY AVAILABLE IN OUR COUNTRIES STILL INCREASES... POLICE ARE LOSING THE DRUG BATTLE WORLDWIDE."

RAYMOND KENDALL,
SECRETARY GENERAL OF INTERPOL
1994

and prevalence of use. The UK, for example, has one of the harshest regimes and the highest level of drug use in Europe[13].

- Different states within the US and Australia have very different enforcement regimes for cannabis possession – from very punitive to de facto decriminalisation. Comparing the different states shows there is no correlation between enforcement and prevalence[14].

- In the UK it is mostly Class A drugs, with the harshest penalties, which have seen the most dramatic rises in use. Heroin use in the UK has risen by at least 1000% since 1971, cocaine use has doubled in the last ten years. Similarly ecstasy use went from zero to several million pills a week being consumed in a matter of years in the late 1980s.

- The Home Office has never undertaken any research to establish the extent of enforcement-related deterrence, despite it being at the heart of the Misuse of Drugs Act and all subsequent policy thinking. The research that does exist suggests enforcement related deterrence is, at best, a marginal factor in influencing decisions to take drugs.

- In his oral evidence to the recent Science and Technology committee, Professor David Nutt, Chairman of the ACMD Technical Committee stated: "I think the evidence base for classification producing a deterrent is not strong".

- The Commons Science and Technology Committee reported that: "We have found no solid evidence to support the existence of a deterrent effect, despite the fact that it appears to underpin the Government's policy on classification"[15].

LIES, DAMNED LIES, STATISTICS, AND LOOK – PROHIBITION WORKS!

Those attempting to defend the status quo, usually those working in government or enforcement, frequently quote statistics that give the misleading impression that prohibition is working – when the exact opposite is true. It is hard to think of another area of social policy where the waters are so muddied by statistical chicanery. This sort of misleading evidence, attempting to dress up failure as success, usually comes in one of five varieties. They are listed below, with some ideas on how to effectively challenge them:

WHY PROHIBITION CAN NEVER WORK

A simple economic analysis can usefully demonstrate why absolute prohibition can never work. Simply put, where high demand exists alongside prohibition, a criminal profit opportunity is inevitably created. Attempts to interrupt criminal drug production and supply are doomed as the effect (if successful – which they very rarely are) will be rising prices; this then makes the market more attractive for new producers and sellers to enter – which they always do. No matter how many dealers we arrest or smuggling networks we 'smash', the void is always filled by the queue of willing replacements, hungry for the extraordinary profits prohibition offers them. Most people will immediately relate to this analysis as it chimes with the experience within their local community.

1. LOCALISED SUCCESS

Example: "Cocaine/heroin production in Colombia/ Afghanistan has fallen this year."

These stats may well be true (they may not, but let's assume they are). However, local production is completely irrelevant in a global market, as falls in production in one region will quickly be made up by rises in another. This pattern has been observed repeatedly in regional shifts in production of coca, opium and cannabis - so frequently that it has become known in official shorthand as 'the balloon effect' (if you squeeze a balloon on one side, it expands on the other). The key point here is that the trend in global production has always kept pace with global demand, which has risen steadily over the past four decades (see: why prohibition can never work, above). Illegal drug markets are not confined by geographical boundaries, and localised successes should not be allowed to disguise larger scale systematic failure to control global production. This is the worst form of cherry-picking. Keep the focus on the bigger picture – using official national and international statistics that are not in dispute (see further information in Chapter 6, p58).

2. SHORT TERM LOCALISED SUCCESS

Example: "Street drug dealing fell by 10% in the last 6 months in Birmingham".

Again, this may well be true – but short-term changes often mask longer-term trends. They can also be due to (non-policy related) external factors, changes in statistical collection or methodology, and sometimes a marginal change can be within statistical error parameters. This sort of cherry picking can also be countered by bringing the focus back to the bigger picture statistics on the failure of the policy nationally and internationally. Be careful to make sure the criticism is aimed at the policy makers, not those who are implementing policy (the police do their job as best they can, it just happens to be an impossible one). Also remind policy makers that it is the policy of prohibition that created the crime and illegal markets in the first place.

3. PROCESS SUCCESS

Examples: "We have set up a new agency, appointed a new Tsar, instigated a partnership project with Jamaican police, invested millions in a, b and c, announced ambitious new targets on x, y and z" etc. etc.

These are age-old exercises in distraction. Policy must be judged on outcomes, not inputs or process indicators. Challenge policy makers on their record: the outcomes of the policies they are supporting. Don't let them get away with announcing yet more headline-grabbing new initiatives. Have these new changes (or "spinitiatives") made any difference to the bigger picture on supply, availability, crime, problematic use? The problems with prohibition are fundamental and cannot be solved with superficial tweaks to policy which, at best, will marginally reduce the harms created by the policy in the first place, and more likely will cost government and taxpayers more money for no benefits.

4. SUCCESS RELATIVE TO PREVIOUS DISASTER:

Example: "crack use has fallen since last year"

When compared to a policy as disastrous as heavy-handed enforcement and large-scale incarceration, almost any change in intervention will start to look like progress. A good example is the improved outcomes from coercing drug-using offenders into abstinence-based 'treatment' as opposed to sending them to jail. The point here is that imprisonment is so expensive and counterproductive that literally any alternative spending would produce better results – burning the money, giving offenders juggling lessons, ANYTHING.

The crack example can also illustrate the important point that drugs come in and out of fashion largely independently of policy and law. Prevalence of one drug may fall after an epidemic (e.g. crack use in the US) whilst another simultaneously rises (in the US this has been methamphetamine). It is relatively easy for policy makers to cherry pick some positive statistics and misleadingly hold them up as representative of wider progress. Again the way to counter this is to focus on the longer-term bigger picture – drug use has risen steadily for decades – especially of the most problematic drugs. If a 'stabilisation' has been 'achieved', this may be sold as a success but most likely it simply reflects a saturated market demand. The UK government has for example been claiming success in the stabilisation of heroin use in the UK over the past 4 or 5 years – it needs to be pointed out that usage has stabilised at the highest level in UK history, the highest level in Europe, and a level approximately 1000% higher than in 1971.

5. SUCCESS ON COMPLETELY MEANINGLESS INDICATORS

Examples: 'volume of drug seizures is up', 'number of dealers jailed has increased', ' we have 'smashed' record numbers of drug gangs' etc.

These are measures that reflect the level of expenditure on enforcement and the size of the illegal market. They rarely, if ever, translate into the policy outputs that prohibition is striving for – i.e. reduced drug production, supply, availability or use (let alone reduced harm). They sound great in the media; catching baddies, intercepting nasty drugs etc – but it gives the misleading impression of success when in reality the opposite is true. Again, challenge people using these sorts of statistics to show what impact they are having on meaningful indicators and keep to the bigger picture. Do not let statements from officials such as talking about 'x quantities of drugs prevented from reaching the streets' go unchallenged. Point out that such seizures have no impact on overall supply and that drugs are cheaper and more available than ever.

Always bring these claims back to the long term ongoing systematic failure of prohibition and the relative effectiveness of regulation against key indicators.

CO-OPTING THE LANGUAGE OF THE DRUG WAR

Many arguments that are made in support of prohibition are easily challenged - prohibition has historically achieved the exact opposite of its stated goals, and tough-talking rhetoric rings very hollow when this is pointed out. When confronted with an unanswerable factual critique of prohibition's failure, its advocates will often retreat behinds 'tough', populist language. This needs to challenged all the more energetically, and there is sometimes a place for co-opting tough-talking populism - especially if it has been used against you - as a way to undermine the prohibitionist paradigm and promote evidence-led public health alternatives.

"POLICIES CONCEIVED AND ENFORCED TO CONTROL DRUG-RELATED PROBLEMS AND EFFECTS HAVE LED TO DISASTROUS AND PERVERSE RESULTS. PROHIBITION IS THE FUNDAMENTAL PRINCIPLE OF DRUG POLICIES. IF WE CONSIDER THE RESULTS ACHIEVED, THERE ARE PROFOUND DOUBTS REGARDING ITS EFFECTIVENESS. PROHIBITIONIST POLICIES HAVE BEEN UNABLE TO CONTROL THE CONSUMPTION OF NARCOTICS; ON THE OTHER HAND, THERE HAS BEEN AN INCREASE OF CRIMINALITY. THERE IS ALSO A HIGH MORTALITY RATE RELATED TO THE QUALITY OF SUBSTANCES AND TO AIDS OR OTHER VIRAL DISEASES."

JORGE SAMPIAIO,
PRESIDENT OF PORTUGAL
MADRID'S EL PAIS, 07.04.97

Some examples; Our policy is "tough on crime" -

- Drug prohibition is not tough on crime - it is manna from heaven for the Mafia, just as it was during alcohol prohibition.

- Prohibition is 'a gangsters charter' - abdicating control of a multi billion pound market in dangerous substances to violent organised criminal networks and unregulated dealers.

- It is organised crime's single biggest source of income, and continues to grow despite the huge enforcement efforts and hundreds of billions spent on the drug war over a number of decades.

- Legally regulating and controlling currently illegal drugs would collapse the illegal markets and get the drug smugglers and dealers out of this business. If we want to really get tough on the drug dealing gangsters let's take away their biggest source of revenue and try to collapse the illegal drug business for good.

Our policy is 'sending out the right message'

- Current drug policy sends out an extremely confused message; one that supports:
  - mass criminalisation of the young and vulnerable

- policies that maximise drug harms such as drug deaths, overdoses and blood borne disease transmission
- ignoring the decades of evidence that shows the policy is a counterproductive failure
- using the blunt tool of criminal justice enforcement to deal with complex social and public health problems
- commercial promotion of dangerous legal drugs

• It can also be pointed out that using criminal law to send out messages about public health or private morality is a bizarre strategy that has been, by any measure, a complete disaster. We do not imprison people for having unsafe sex, or other consenting adult risk taking behaviours such as dangerous sports, or for that matter, legal drug use. Homosexuality was legalised when the unacceptable injustice of imposing private morality with criminal law was exposed.

• Moves toward regulation and control, by contrast, send out the message that:

- we are rationally looking at the evidence of what works
- we are anti-illegal markets and gangsterism, genuinely tough on crime
- we think that public health problems should be dealt with as such
- we care about protecting the young and vulnerable, and providing appropriate help where needed
- we are going to show leadership and not be bullied into continuing with failed and counterproductive policies just to appease some international partners/agencies (primarily the US and UN drug agencies), or the tabloid press
- (see also 'morals and messages' p.52)

> **"I SAY LEGALISE DRUGS BECAUSE I WANT TO SEE LESS DRUG ABUSE, NOT MORE. AND I SAY LEGALISE DRUGS BECAUSE I WANT TO SEE THE CRIMINALS PUT OUT OF BUSINESS."**
>
> **EDWARD ELLISON,**
> **OPERATIONAL HEAD OF SCOTLAND YARD'S DRUGS SQUAD,1982- 86**
> **TRANSFORM PATRON**
> **DAILY MAIL 10.03.98**

'Drugs are dangerous and must be controlled'

• Exactly right. But the drug war concept of 'controlled drugs' is an absurdity, because prohibition has abdicated all control of drugs to gangsters. Control of drugs under prohibition is demonstrably impossible. In reality it leads to a complete lack of control and creates criminal anarchy.

• Real control means taking the markets back from criminal networks and bringing them within the government sphere, where drug production, supply and use can be regulated, as strictly as is deemed appropriate for each drug in any given locale .

• It is precisely because drugs are dangerous that they need to be regulated and controlled.

• Drugs are too dangerous to be left in the hands of criminals.

• The more dangerous a drug is, the more important that it is properly controlled by the government.

• Drugs are made even more dangerous when produced and supplied through illegal channels.

"PLEASE CAN WE BEGIN TO HEAR SOME GOOD SENSE FROM NO 10 AND THE HOME OFFICE, AND LET'S START LOOKING AT HOW DRUGS CAN BE LEGALISED AND OUR SOCIETY CAN BE DECRIMINALISED. LET'S RECOGNISE REALITY AND START TO REDUCE THE NUMBERS WHO ARE CLUTTERING UP OUR PRISONS. LET'S START SELLING DRUGS THROUGH OUTLETS SUCH AS OFF-LICENCES, WHERE THE LIKELIHOOD OF DEALING WITH SOMEONE HOLDING A GUN IS VIRTUALLY ZERO, UNLIKE THE STREET TRADERS OF TODAY. LET'S ADMIT THAT WE ARE GETTING IT WRONG, BY ALLOWING OUR FEAR AND PREJUDICE AGAINST CERTAIN DRUGS TO DRIVE US TO PURSUE WRONGHEADED POLICIES WHICH ONLY PRODUCE DAMAGING SOCIAL RESULTS."

MO MOWLAM,
FORMER MP, CABINET MINISTER FROM 1997-2001,
RESPONSIBLE FOR THE GOVERNMENT'S DRUGS POLICY FROM 1999-2001.

"BETTER DRUGS LAWS WILL CUT GUN CRIME -
LET'S RECOGNISE REALITY AND START SELLING THE STUFF AT OFF-LICENCES"
THE GUARDIAN 09.01.03

4. MAKING THE CASE FOR REGULATED MARKETS

ALTHOUGH IT IS IMPORTANT TO EXPOSE THE SHORTCOMINGS OF CURRENT DRUG POLICY, NO AMOUNT OF DEVASTATING CRITIQUE OF PROHIBITION WILL ACHIEVE VERY MUCH UNLESS A CONVINCING CASE FOR AN ALTERNATIVE POLICY IS MADE. THE BIG PROBLEM WITH THE SO-CALLED 'LEGALISATION LOBBY' IN THE PAST IS THAT BRILLIANT CRITIQUE HAS TENDED TO BE FOLLOWED WITH A ONE WORD SOLUTION – 'LEGALISATION'. THIS CHAPTER CONSIDERS HOW TO ADVOCATE CLEARLY WHAT THE REPLACEMENT FOR PROHIBITION WILL LOOK LIKE, AND THE PRINCIPLES BY WHICH SUCH POLICY ALTERNATIVES WILL BE DEVELOPED AND IMPLEMENTED. THE NEXT CHAPTER CONSIDERS A NUMBER OF THE MOST COMMON CONCERNS RAISED ABOUT A POST-PROHIBITION WORLD, AND HOW THESE CONCERNS CAN BE ADDRESSED.

"NO ONE IS ASKING FOR SOME FREE-FOR-ALL FOR DRUGS. I WANT DRUGS TO BE CONTROLLED AND REGULATED, BUT WE DO NOT WANT TO ALLOW WHAT HAS HAPPENED OVER THE PAST THIRTY YEARS TO CONTINUE, WHEREBY, IN AN ILLEGAL MARKET, CRIMINALS – IRRESPONSIBLE PEOPLE – SELL POISONED DRUGS THAT KILL YOUNG PEOPLE"

PAUL FLYNN MP

FROM 'LEGALISATION' TO 'REGULATION'

The alternative to the current system of drug prohibition needs to be clearly and confidently specified. Just saying 'legalisation' is inadequate - and indeed problematic, as the term comes with a lot of baggage. For many people it is associated with either 'hippies and pot-heads', specific political ideologies (usually libertarianism or liberalism) that condone the use of drugs, or suggests a 'surrender' in the drug war that would leave us with some sort of un-policed 'free for all'. Using the term in isolation creates a vacuum that will be filled by such misconceptions (which are regularly promoted by prohibition's advocates and political beneficiaries[16]) – frequently of the 'heroin would be available in sweet shops' variety.

In actuality the term 'legalisation' describes a process (rather like 'abolition')- in this case the process of something currently illegal being made legal – rather than an end point or goal in itself. It gives no indication what the policy replacing prohibition would look like. For this reason it is very important that the term is clarified as soon and often as possible.

Explain what you mean by 'legalisation' at the earliest opportunity and try to talk about 'regulation and control' as often as possible. There is no harm in repeating the phrase – in fact we would encourage it. Avoiding the term 'legalisation' altogether is no bad thing, but if it is unavoidable, either use it in the phrase 'legalisation and regulation' or make it clear it is a process not an end point: 'legalisation is necessary to move from prohibition to legally regulated markets'. A useful alternative is to talk about 'moves towards legal regulation and control', or 'legally regulated drug markets'.

BE CLEAR ABOUT WHAT REGULATED MARKETS ARE, AND WHAT THEY ARE NOT

Once you have clarified that your understanding of 'legalisation' is very specifically 'regulation and control', whenever possible it is worth going further to explain in very clear terms more precisely what you are proposing and the principles on which future policy developments would be based.

- Some activities and products would remain prohibited as part of the regulatory framework.

This is hugely important point to make as it reinforces the idea of control, and moves perceptions away from the misconceptions of 'legalisation' and libertarian free markets. Activities that would remain prohibited would include, for example, underage sales, consumption in public, unlicensed sales, advertising and so on. Similarly, supply of certain particularly potent or high risk preparations of some drugs would also remain prohibited. All psychoactive drugs are potentially dangerous substances that should be subject to tight legal and social regulations. We should learn the lessons from tobacco and alcohol (see – 'talking about... alcohol and tobacco' p.37). The level of enforcement, and associated penalties for activities that remain prohibited, would be determined by legislation, police force or local licensing body as appropriate. Discussing the role of 'prohibitions' post legalisation may be a bit confusing; to avoid this, talk about replacing 'absolute prohibition' or 'the war on drugs' with 'a system of strict legal regulation and control in which some activities remain prohibited'.

"ONLY LEGALISING THE MOST WIDELY USED DRUGS, SUBJECTING THEM TO STRICT QUALITY ASSESSMENT AND MAKING THEM AVAILABLE THROUGH CONTROLLED OUTLETS, WILL ALLOW PEOPLE TO MAKE INTELLIGENT CHOICES.

THE MOST ODIOUS TYRANNIES ARE THOSE THAT SEEK TO IMPOSE UNREAL VALUES ON SOCIETY. DRUGS POLICY HAS BECOME SUCH A TYRANNY. THE HARD TRUTH IS THAT MILLIONS OF PEOPLE WANT THE FREEDOM TO USE DRUGS, AND NO POLICY OF PROHIBITION IS GOING TO STOP THEM. ISN'T IT TIME GOVERNMENT ACCEPTED THIS FACT, AND ALLOWED THEM TO USE DRUGS MORE SAFELY AND AT LESS RISK TO OTHERS?"

PROFESSOR JOHN GRAY,
PROFESSOR OF EUROPEAN THOUGHT AT THE LONDON SCHOOL OF ECONOMICS
'INJECTING SOME SENSE - MILLIONS OF PEOPLE WANT TO USE DRUGS AND PROHIBITION WILL NOT STOP THEM'
THE GUARDIAN 10.07.01

- Make it clear you are not talking about a free market that would give carte blanche to multinationals and pharmaceutical companies to market or promote recreational drugs (see 'concerns about legalisation/regulation' p.46). Producers would be strictly regulated, particularly with regard to advertising, marketing, health warnings and packaging.

- Different regulatory regimes would be put in place for different drugs in different locations. The strictness of regulation for different drugs (or different preparations of a given drug) would be determined by the comparative risks associated with their production, supply and use.

- Regulatory regimes would be based on existing models (something people can immediately understand) including;

  - Medical prescription (possibly involving supervised use) for the most risky drugs (e.g. injectable heroin - the legal framework for which already exists in practice)

  - Over the counter pharmacy sales - from qualified pharmacists (possibly with additional training for vending recreational drugs)

  - Licensed sales (as with off licenses or tobacconists) with various available tiers of licensing conditions that could be applied as appropriate

  - Licensed premises (pubs or Dutch style coffee-shops) again, with variable licensing conditions.

  - Unlicensed sales for low risk drugs - like coffee

(for more discussion of regulatory models see the Transform, KCBA and HOBC reports detailed in Chapter 6, p.59).

- The type of regulation for each drug would be based on evidence of what works. Unlike the inflexible straitjacket of prohibition, a regulatory regime could develop a range of responses to the risks that different drugs present. Different models would be piloted and tested, with policy development and implementation based on evidence of effectiveness. Regulatory frameworks could be changed and updated in response to changing circumstances.

• Implementation would be phased and based on the precautionary principle. Regulated models would not be rolled out for all drugs overnight. It is likely that certain drugs would be legalised and regulated first (probably cannabis) and other drugs phased in over a number of years. Initially the default position would be to err on the side of stricter regulation, which could then be relaxed only if evidence suggested that would be more effective.

• Internationally, this is about returning democratic freedoms to sovereign states. Under this new system no country is going to be bullied into legalising and regulating any drug (in contrast to the bullying to maintain prohibition that many experience now). The changes we are seeking at the international level would change the UN legal system to allow the freedom of individual states to democratically decide on any move towards regulated drug markets if they determined that was the best way forward for them. It would merely put regulatory policy options back in the frame. If certain nation states (those, perhaps, where alcohol is still prohibited) wished to maintain absolute prohibition, that decision would remain their sovereign right.

RE-ESTABLISHING THE PRIMACY OF A PUBLIC HEALTH / HARM REDUCTION APPROACH

Once the meaning of control and regulation is made clear, it becomes much easier to grasp that the response to illegal drugs need not be any different to our current response to legal drugs (see 'fault-lines within existing policy' p.15), or for that matter any other issue in the public health arena. Making the case for a public health-led response is crucial to getting the reform message across. It is a concept people are familiar with and understand (in relation to, for example, tobacco policy), and it helps direct the emphasis of the discourse towards evidence-based policy making and harm reduction – and away from the ideological dream of achieving a 'drug free society'.

• The fact that certain drugs are currently dealt with via the criminal justice system is a quirk of the history of prohibition, and not the conclusion of any kind of rational analysis or evaluation. Drugs, quite simply, are primarily a public heath issue and should be dealt with as such by the relevant public health agencies (see principles of drug policy – p.20).

• Prohibition not only undermines public health efforts to reduce drug harm (by diverting budgets to enforcement and stigmatising the most vulnerable problem users with criminality) it actually increases harms associated with use by encouraging high risk behaviours (e.g. injecting/sharing needles), stifles access to accurate safety information, and ensures that dangerous drugs are of unknown strength and purity.

• Public health interventions have beeen shown to be effective (e.g. needle exchanges, treatment programmes, controls on tobacco advertising), criminal justice interventions generally have not.

• Illegal drugs are unique in the public health arena in attempting to use criminal law as the primary method of educating the public. We have a whole range of alternative methods for public health education in schools, workplaces, public spaces, media and the home that can be shown

> "THE CURRENT ARRANGEMENTS TO CONTROL THE SUPPLY OF ILLEGAL DRUGS SHOULD BE REVIEWED TO DETERMINE WHETHER ANY COST-EFFECTIVE AND POLITICALLY ACCEPTABLE MEASURES CAN BE TAKEN TO REDUCE THEIR AVAILABILITY TO YOUNG PEOPLE"
>
> THE ADVISORY COUNCIL ON THE MISUSE OF DRUGS
> RECOMMENDATION FROM 'PATHWAYS TO PROBLEMS' REPORT 14.09.06

to be more effective (and don't involve making criminals out of a third of the country).

If the case for a public health-led response can be made effectively, it can only lead in one direction – away from ideological prohibition and towards evidence based regulation and control. Once you have people thinking along these lines you are well on the way to winning them over.

YOU CAN BE ANTI-DRUG AND PRO-REFORM

As has been discussed elsewhere in the guide (p.19), the way the drugs debate has historically been framed often leads to pro-reform positions being confused with (or misrepresented as) being 'pro-drug' or somehow condoning, encouraging or giving approval for drug use generally. Without rehashing the same material covered elsewhere, it is vital to emphasise that support for principled, phased, evidence led reform of failed drug legislation is in no way incompatible with a strong anti-drug message, or the moral view that a drug-free lifestyle is to be encouraged.

It is often useful to make this point explicitly. It defuses potential accusations about 'sending out the wrong message', especially if you are crystal clear about your message on drug use / misuse, and the mechanisms by which you would like to see that message 'sent out' (i.e. through proven public education channels, rather than discredited criminal justice ones). In many respects prohibition is an active obstacle to effective public health messages, directing resources away from education and prevention into enforcement, whilst simultaneously alienating young people and fostering distrust of government messages on drugs through blanket criminalisation. To defend prohibition is to send far more confusing messages: defending organised crime's biggest business, and guaranteeing that the harm caused by drugs will be maximised.

KEEPING THE FOCUS ON THE INTERNATIONAL DIMENSION

It is important to remember that how we respond to the drugs issue in the UK has a direct impact on the rest of the world. It is a much overlooked fact in the drugs debate that the impact of our domestic policies go way beyond British shores. We have to be wary of not slipping into a parochial perspective on this issue.

- Illegal production of drugs consumed in the West now form a significant proportion of the economies in key producer and transit countries such as Afghanistan, Colombia and Jamaica. The vast quantities of illegal profits accruing to violent gangsters and criminal cartels are a significant factor undermining the social, economic and political stability of communities and entire nations across the globe.

- Illegal drug profits are used to corrupt officials at all levels of politics: judiciary, police and military.

- Illegal drug profits are helping to fund and arm paramilitary groups, guerrilla groups, and terrorist organisations across the globe, fuelling and escalating violence in already unstable conflict zones.

These problems are a direct consequence of the policy of prohibition. Blaming drugs or drug users is just a distraction, as the lack of such problems associated with alcohol and tobacco demonstrates.

Just as prohibition is enshrined in international law, so the reform movement must engage in the international arena to tackle the challenges presented by the UN drug conventions and the agencies that oversee them. The international consensus is heavily underpinned by the USA, which played the leading role in developing international drug prohibition in the 1950's and whose institutions and funding still remain its most powerful bulwark. Challenging US hegemony of the UN drug agencies remains key to unlocking the rigid framework of international prohibition.

We need to be wary of being labelled with 'anti-Americanism' by making it clear that it is the USA's drug policies we are critical of, not the country itself or its people. It is also worth highlighting that there is a vibrant and growing domestic US-based reform movement for you to draw upon, part of a wider coalition of reform-minded organisations and individuals operating around the world. And indeed every time the question of drug policy reform has been put to the American people – usually in the form of state propositions to decriminalise cannabis for medical use – they have supported it, only to be overruled by their federal government. It is hard to ignore the symmetry between the US's heavy-handed global policing and the bullying tactics to which it increasingly has to resort to maintain global drug prohibition; but it is important to remember that the US has a vital role to play in global reform and needs to be engaged with the same intelligence and sensitivity as other key audiences.

TALKING ABOUT... ALCOHOL AND TOBACCO

There are many important lessons for us to draw from the successes and failures with legal regulation of alcohol and tobacco. These will inevitably crop up and it is useful to have a grasp of the key arguments so that you can turn any mention of currently legal drugs to your advantage. (see also: The fault lines within current policy, p.15).

"PROHIBITION IS NO MORE A VIABLE POLICY IN BRITAIN TODAY THAN IT PROVED TO BE IN AMERICA DURING THE 1920S AND 1930S."

RSA REPORT
'DRUGS: FACING FACTS" 2007

Both tobacco and alcohol are often talked of as if they are not 'real drugs' - or sometimes not drugs at all, underlined by the frequent use of daft phrases such as 'alcohol and drugs', which is about as logical as saying 'orange juice and drinks' or 'sandals and footwear'. Obviously both alcohol and tobacco are powerful psychoactive drugs; potentially highly toxic, addictive and associated with high mortality rates. Were they to be classified under the current policy regime (the Misuse of Drugs Act 1971) they would certainly be class A or B. Do not hesitate to point this fact out[17].

> **"IT IS SALUTARY TO SEE THAT ALCOHOL AND TOBACCO-THE MOST WIDELY USED UNCLASSIFIED SUBSTANCES-WOULD HAVE HARM RATINGS COMPARABLE WITH CLASS A AND B ILLEGAL DRUGS, RESPECTIVELY."**
>
> **DAVID NUTT, LESLIE KING, WILLIAM SAULSBURY, COLIN BLAKEMORE, THE LANCET, MARCH 2007**

However, for reasons that have no bearing on any scientific assessment of actual risk, harmfulness or danger, tobacco and alcohol are both legally produced, supplied and consumed, albeit within a regulatory framework within which some prohibitions remain (failings of this system are discussed below). The distinction between legal and illegal drugs is not justifiable under any scientific, logical or public health criteria and is purely an artefact of quirks in our social and political history. The argument that 'it's not fair' people are allowed to use one drug and not another is a strong one – but it needs to be deployed carefully (see 'Talking about...personal rights' p.43).

For all the health and social problems associated with alcohol and tobacco use, the key difference with illegal drugs is on the production and supply side. Alcohol and tobacco are produced under licence and under the law, are liable to taxation, regulation and inspection, alcohol is sold in licensed shops and premises (tobacco is unlicensed but subject to age of purchaser controls), tobacco products (and soon alcohol products) provide information on strength and health warnings on the packaging. We have none of the criminal market problems that we have for currently illegal drugs (see tobacco notes below re: illicit smuggling).

HOUSE OF COMMONS BRANDED WISKEY

It is entirely consistent to call for more regulation of alcohol and tobacco as well as the legalisation and regulation of currently illegal drugs. This is about applying the same evidence-led public health and harm reduction principles to all drugs, and developing the optimum level of regulation for each.

TOBACCO

- The high prevalence of tobacco use is due to a number of factors including its long history of use, its aggressive promotion as an aspirational lifestyle product over the last century, and the nature of nicotine intoxication that enables people to function normally at the same time as being addicted, lending itself to long-term high-frequency use.

- Increasingly effective regulation of tobacco (including recent bans on advertising and smoking in public spaces) and, more importantly, growing public understanding of the negative health consequences of smoking backed up with comparatively well funded health education campaigns on the risks of smoking - have all led to a steady reduction in smoking over the past three decades. Admittedly this was from a very high point in the post war era, before which advertising was aggressive and unfettered, and the medical consequences of smoking poorly understood. Nevertheless, it does illustrate how prevalence of a legal drug can change positively in response to sensible regulation and public health education. There is clearly some distance to go: tobacco sales remain effectively unlicensed and key concepts in tobacco harm reduction (such as smokeless tobacco products) have yet to trouble UK policy makers.

- The illegal market in smuggled tobacco is the direct result of taxation policy - specifically the large international differentials in tobacco tax that create a huge profit opportunity for smugglers. For example, tax rates on tobacco vary from zero percent in Andorra, to several hundred percent in the UK – a far greater range than almost any other mass consumer product. If tobacco taxes were reduced domestically, the international differential and profit opportunity in smuggling and illicit sales would fall accordingly; where there is no tobacco tax there are no smuggled imports or illicit sales. Higher taxes, however, mean higher prices which can effectively dissuade potential new users and encourage existing users to quit, just as falling prices can have the opposite effect. The government has the difficult task of using taxation policy to balance these two conflicting needs (dissuading use / undermining illegal activity). Crucially, though, because tobacco is legal and regulated, governments are in a position of power to intervene on price, an impossibility with illegal drugs that are entirely at the whim of supply and demand in an unregulated criminal market. It is also worth noting that most smuggled tobacco is at least legally produced in the first instance.

"THE PRESTIGE OF GOVERNMENT HAS UNDOUBTEDLY BEEN LOWERED CONSIDERABLY BY THE PROHIBITION LAW. FOR NOTHING IS MORE DESTRUCTIVE OF RESPECT FOR THE GOVERNMENT AND THE LAW OF THE LAND THAN PASSING LAWS WHICH CANNOT BE ENFORCED. IT IS AN OPEN SECRET THAT THE DANGEROUS INCREASE OF CRIME IN THIS COUNTRY IS CLOSELY CONNECTED WITH THIS."

PROFESSOR ALBERT EINSTEIN,
NOBEL LAUREATE (PHYSICS)
MY FIRST IMPRESSION OF THE U.S.A.', 1921
(QUOTE IN REFERENCE TO US ALCOHOL PROHIBITION)

- It is worth noting that the profit margins on illegal drugs are so high, often running to 1000% or more, that there is plenty of room for manoeuvre for policy makers regarding tax and price control interventions. Prohibition has turned heroin and cocaine – essentially low value processed agricultural products - into illicit commodities literally worth more than their weight in gold. Even with high taxes, legally supplied drugs would still dramatically undercut current illicit markets.

ALCOHOL

- Prevalence of alcohol use is high (relative to illegal drugs) because it is the oldest and most culturally established of all drugs, and its use is deeply embedded into a wide range of pleasurable and sociable contexts. The prevalence of problematic alcohol use and risky patterns of consumption (heavy, frequent or binge drinking) along with related crime and disorder problems are getting worse (in the UK) partly because of social and cultural changes and partly due to poor regulation of supply and a lack of effective public health education.

> "WITH NEARLY ONE IN FIVE BRITONS AGED 20 TO 24 NOW USING CANNABIS REGULARLY, IT'S CLEAR THAT THE CURRENT LAW IS USELESS AS A DETERRENT AND SERVES ONLY TO CRIMINALISE OTHERWISE LAW-ABIDING PEOPLE WHILE EATING UP VAST AMOUNTS OF POLICE TIME."
>
> NEW SCIENTIST MAGAZINE, EDITORIAL 03.10.02

- Alcohol can still be advertised with few restrictions, and is often directly marketed to young people and children through sport sponsorship such as Premiership football and Formula 1 racing. Sums of money spent on public health education are eclipsed by spending on advertising and promotion. New alcohol products are being developed and marketed (such as 'alcopops') that actively target younger emerging markets and encourage risky patterns of use, despite implausible claims to the contrary from the alcohol industry.

- If problematic alcohol use is to be tackled there must be far stricter controls over advertising, marketing and promotion - starting with minimum prices and a ban on sports and youth events sponsorship, perhaps leading to an outright advertising ban, similar to that on tobacco. Far greater investment must be made in effective targeted health education (something the Government's own appointed expert advisors agree with[11]). These are both policies that would surely apply to any legalised and regulated drug in the future. We will never have to suffer Cocaine Premiership Football or Ecstasy World Snooker.

- With alcohol we have a unique and unambiguous example of where prohibition was tried (in the US 1920-1933) failed horribly (for the same reasons drug prohibition is failing now) and was ultimately repealed.

TALKING ABOUT... CANNABIS

Cannabis is the most widely used illegal drug by a large margin, and has correspondingly dominated the debate on drug law reform for decades. Levels of support for cannabis decriminalisation/legalisation have risen from around 15% in the 1980s to consistently over 50% today[7], despite a large scale domestic and international propaganda effort to hype the drug's undoubted potential dangers: this is an extremely positive precedent for the drug reform movement as a whole. What is clear is that exposure to informed debate on the drugs issue invariably pushes opinion away from prohibition and towards reform.

However, there are problems with how the cannabis debate has been handled historically that mean caution needs to be taken when approaching it.

- Saying cannabis should be legalised and regulated 'because it's safe' is neither true nor useful. Like all drugs cannabis has risks and even if they are relatively low, a minority of vulnerable users do run into real problems with it. Claiming otherwise is every bit as foolish and unscientific as some of the more outlandish 'reefer madness' claims made by advocates of its continued prohibition. This line of argument also undermines the wider argument for drug law reform; It is because drugs are dangerous / risky that they need to be properly regulated. You can go further to say that the more dangerous a drug is the more imperative it becomes to legally regulate it, and take it out of the hands of criminals.

- In this sense the cannabis debate dominates the wider drugs debate in a way that grossly overstates its importance, and it has become a distraction from more important issues. The essentially trivial dispute over cannabis reclassification hogged media and parliamentary debate for nearly two years - during which time more substantive debates on how to address the dramatic failings of the drug strategy, and how it was fuelling crime, prison overcrowding and the wider crisis in the criminal justice system, were largely overlooked. When the issue of cannabis comes up, try to move the debate to policy on all drugs.

- The debate around recreational cannabis use often gets entangled with the debate around its medical use, and occasionally with the commercial/industrial use of the hemp plant. Since the arguments for the recreational, medical and industrial uses of the plant are very different, they are not usefully combined - try to keep them separate. The fact cannabis (or its extracts) can be a useful medicine, for example, doesn't have the slightest relevance to its recreational risk profile. Remember that we are concerned here with the drug's recreational use only.

None of this is to say that you shouldn't discuss the cannabis issue at all: it will invariably come up, so it is good to be prepared. It can be useful to get people thinking about the wider issues of drug law reform, especially since there is a substantial constituency of people who support legalisation of cannabis but not other drugs. Given that exactly the same arguments apply – reducing harms and protecting freedoms of individuals – it is easy to challenge the substantial 'cannabis yes – but not the rest' audience in a way that forces them to think about the bigger picture. Cannabis is also unique in that in many countries positive reform is already underway. This provides useful debating resource where such policies can be shown to be effective, particularly in the case of Holland, where the drug is de facto decriminalised, regulated and tolerated.

TALKING ABOUT... CRACK COCAINE

'OK – but what about Crack?' : it crops up all the time. It's an understandable question – how do we deal sensibly with the drug with the worst reputation for chaos and danger? The answer, as elsewhere, is to begin by moving beyond the denial stage: the fantasy that this is a problem that can be eradicated with criminal justice enforcement. However distasteful, we need to accept the reality that some people use crack; then we need to consider the evidence of what interventions are going to be effective at reducing the harm crack causes to users and the wider community.

"WE SUPPORT THE RUNCIMAN INQUIRY'S RECOMMENDATIONS THAT "THE POSSESSION OF CANNABIS SHOULD NOT BE AN IMPRISONABLE OFFENCE." WE ALSO WISH TO SUPPORT SOME OF THE COGENT ARGUMENT OF PETER LILLEY MP...WHERE HE SAYS THAT INEBRIATION IS REGARDED AS A SIN BECAUSE IT CAN LEAD TO MORE SERIOUS WRONGDOING. ALCOHOL INEBRIATION HAS LONG BEEN ASSOCIATED WITH VIOLENCE IN SOME CASES, AND IT IS POSSIBLE THAT CANNABIS ABUSE COULD SOMETIMES HAVE HARMFUL EFFECTS. HOWEVER THAT IS A MATTER FOR PERSONAL RESPONSIBILITY, GUIDED BY MORAL IMPERATIVES. ABUSE, WHICH IS A SIN, IS NOT NECESSARILY A CRIME".

CHURCH OF ENGLAND BOARD FOR SOCIAL RESPONSIBILITY
WRITTEN SUBMISSION TO THE HOME AFFAIRS SELECT COMMITTEE 2001

"IF IT WERE ABSOLUTELY ESTABLISHED THAT THERE WAS A HIGHER ADDICTION RATE WITH CRACK, LEGALIZATION COULD, PARADOXICALLY, DIMINISH ITS USE. THIS IS SO BECAUSE IF COCAINE WERE REDUCED TO THE SAME PRICE AS CRACK, THE ABUSER, ACKNOWLEDGING THE HIGHER RATE OF ADDICTION, MIGHT FORGO THE MORE INTENSIVE HIGH OF CRACK, OPTING FOR THE SLOWER HIGH OF COCAINE. CRACK WAS INTRODUCED YEARS AGO AS OFFERING AN ALLURING NEW PSYCHO ACTIVE EXPERIENCE. BUT ITS SPECIAL HOLD ON THE GHETTO IS THE RESULT OF ITS PRICE. REMEMBER THAT—ON ANOTHER FRONT—WE KNOW THAT 120-PROOF ALCOHOL DOESN'T SELL AS READILY AS 86 PROOF, NOT BY A LONG SHOT, EVEN THOUGH THE HIGHER THE PROOF, THE FASTER THE PSYCHOLOGICAL EFFECT THAT ALCOHOL USERS ARE SEEKING."

PROFESSOR MICHAEL GAZZANIGA
PROFESSOR OF PSYCHIATRY AT DARTMOUTH MEDICAL SCHOOL, EDITOR-IN-CHIEF OF THE JOURNAL OF COGNITIVE NEUROSCIENCE
THE NATIONAL REVIEW FEBRUARY 05.02.90

THE RESPONSE MUST BE PUBLIC HEALTH LED AND BASED ON HARM REDUCTION PRINCIPLES

Public health interventions are far harder for crack than for heroin. While even the most chaotic heroin users will respond to regular prescriptions that satisfy their needs, crack users will often binge frequently and uncontrollably. While heroin users may accept substitute prescriptions such as methadone, no such alternatives for crack exist (although some have been suggested and research continues, including prescribing of substitute stimulants and development of less potent, slower releasing cocaine preparations). New challenges are emerging as patterns of drug use shift and change – this is a rapidly evolving field.

The simplest option would be for powder cocaine to be sold or prescribed from specialist pharmacy outlets under certain strict conditions, (prescribing cocaine is already possible in the UK, so no change in the law would be required - although prescribing guidelines would need updating).

Since making smokable crack cocaine from powder cocaine is a simple kitchen procedure, and one that is impossible to prevent, so dedicated crack users may continue to procure it, even if it were not directly available. Ultimately, however, the pragmatic reality remains that if someone is determined enough to use crack it is preferable that they have a supply of known strength and purity and do not have to commit crimes against others or prostitute themselves as a means to buying it.

It is also well established from the experience with heroin prescribing that bringing problem users into contact with services through a prescription regime increases the likelihood that they will use those services, enter treatment or rehab, and move away from problematic use altogether.

"PERSISTING IN OUR CURRENT POLICIES WILL ONLY RESULT IN MORE DRUG ABUSE, MORE EMPOWERMENT OF DRUG MARKETS AND CRIMINALS, AND MORE DISEASE AND SUFFERING. TOO OFTEN THOSE WHO CALL FOR OPEN DEBATE, RIGOROUS ANALYSIS OF CURRENT POLICIES, AND SERIOUS CONSIDERATION OF ALTERNATIVES ARE ACCUSED OF "SURRENDERING." BUT THE TRUE SURRENDER IS WHEN FEAR AND INERTIA COMBINE TO SHUT OFF DEBATE, SUPPRESS CRITICAL ANALYSIS, AND DISMISS ALL ALTERNATIVES TO CURRENT POLICIES. MR. SECRETARY GENERAL, WE APPEAL TO YOU TO INITIATE A TRULY OPEN AND HONEST DIALOGUE REGARDING THE FUTURE OF GLOBAL DRUG CONTROL POLICIES - ONE IN WHICH FEAR, PREJUDICE AND PUNITIVE PROHIBITIONS YIELD TO COMMON SENSE, SCIENCE, PUBLIC HEALTH AND HUMAN RIGHTS."

FROM 1998 LETTER TO KOFI ANNAN
SIGNED BY OVER 500 PROMIENT ACADEMICS, SCIENTISTS AND POLITICAL LEADERS INCLUDING:

PROFESSOR COLIN BLAKEMORE
PRESIDENT, BRITISH ASSOCIATION FOR THE ADVANCEMENT OF SCIENCE

ROWAN WILLIAMS,
ARCHBISHOP CANTERBURY (THEN BISHOP OF MONMOTH)

Problem crack users are at the hard end of chaotic drug use and cause a disproportionate amount of secondary harms to society. There is no benefit in further criminalising and demonising them when what is clearly required is a concerted public health response combined with appropriate social support.

'What about crack?' is also a question that highlights the role of prohibition in the emergence of the 'crack epidemic'. The unregulated economics of illegal markets under prohibition always tend to cause concentration of available drug preparations which are more profitable per unit weight. Just as under alcohol prohibition the trade in beer gave way to more concentrated, profitable and dangerous spirits, the same pattern has been observed over the past century with opiates – from opium (smoked or in drinkable preparations) to injectable heroin, and more recently with the cannabis market being increasingly saturated with more potent varieties. With coca-based products the transformation has been dramatic. Before its prohibition, the common forms of cocaine use were low-risk coca leaf chewing and coca-based drinks (tea and wine). It was prohibition that brought cocaine powder onto the streets in the first place, and finally produced high-risk smokable crack[18]. We have prohibition to thank for crack: a powerful reason for ending it before it generates new and even more dangerous drugs

The market for cocaine is currently defined by the fact that only the strongest and most dangerous forms of the drug are available. If less potent preparations were available, demand would be likely to move away from the more risky preparations, just as patterns of alcohol use shifted back towards beers and wines when US alcohol prohibition was repealed. In the case of crack cocaine in the UK, the long-established illegal heroin market created a ready made distribution network and receptive user base for the new product. The heroin and crack markets have meshed within a comparatively short period (most crack users are also heroin users). If these illegal networks were dismantled through the introduction of regulated supply, we would dramatically reduce the possibility for the next new drug 'epidemic', meth-amphetamine perhaps, to take hold.

TALKING ABOUT... PERSONAL RIGHTS

The arguments for the personal right to use drugs are strong. They are based on the principles of John Stuart Mill that underpin most modern lawmaking: that consenting adults should be free to engage in whatever behaviour they wish as long as it does not harm others, and that acting in order to prevent the individual from harming themselves is not legitimate. Indeed, there are no comparable laws in the UK against self-harm, up to and including the legalisation of suicide in 1961. People are free to indulge in all manner of risky and harmful activities including dangerous sports, unsafe sex, and of course legal drug use including alcohol and tobacco (responsible for tens of thousands of deaths each year). Drug laws that criminalise personal use (technically, possession for personal use) are significantly at odds with the law as it applies to comparable personal choices. They are also entirely different to laws that, rightly, criminalise harming others such as rape, theft, murder etc. Do highlight this obvious distinction if you hear the somewhat desperate prohibitionist argument along the lines of: "well why not legalise murder?"

Liberty are among the civil rights groups who agree with this and have a specific policy calling for an end to total prohibition.

Unfortunately, whilst this argument may carry weight intellectually, it carries very little politically or with public opinion. Policy makers, perhaps understandably with so many other battles to fight, are simply not going to risk political capital campaigning for the right to take drugs. Similarly, public opinion is unlikely to be won over rapidly on this one, with the media focusing almost exclusively on the negative aspects of drug use. So realistically, in the short term at least, it is rarely useful to push this part of the reform argument. Respond appropriately if it is raised but, unless absolutely necessary, don't bother raising it unless you have an obviously receptive audience.

If this argument is going to make any real progress in the short term it will be in the courts, when unjust prosecutions or laws are challenged under human rights legislation, as has already begun to happen in mainland Europe.

> **"LIBERTY CONSIDERS THAT THE CURRENT POLICY OF CRIMINALISATION OF POSSESSION, USE AND SUPPLY OF DRUGS REPRESENTS SERIOUS INFRINGEMENTS INTO CIVIL LIBERTIES THAT ARE UNJUSTIFIED. LIBERTY THEREFORE CALLS FOR THE GENERAL DECRIMINALISATION OF POSSESSION, USE AND SUPPLY AND SUPPLY OF ALL DRUGS, FOR THE REGIME FOR CONTROL OF DRUGS TO BE REPLACED BY A CIVIL MECHANISM OF CONTROL, AND FOR THERE TO BE RIGHT OF ACCESS TO THE LAWFUL SUPPLY OF DRUGS."**
>
> NATIONAL COUNCIL FOR CIVIL LIBERTIES
>
> FROM WRITTEN SUBMISSION TO THE HOME AFFAIRS SELECT COMMITTEE INQUIRY 'THE GOVERNMENT'S DRUG POLICY: IS IT WORKING?' 2001

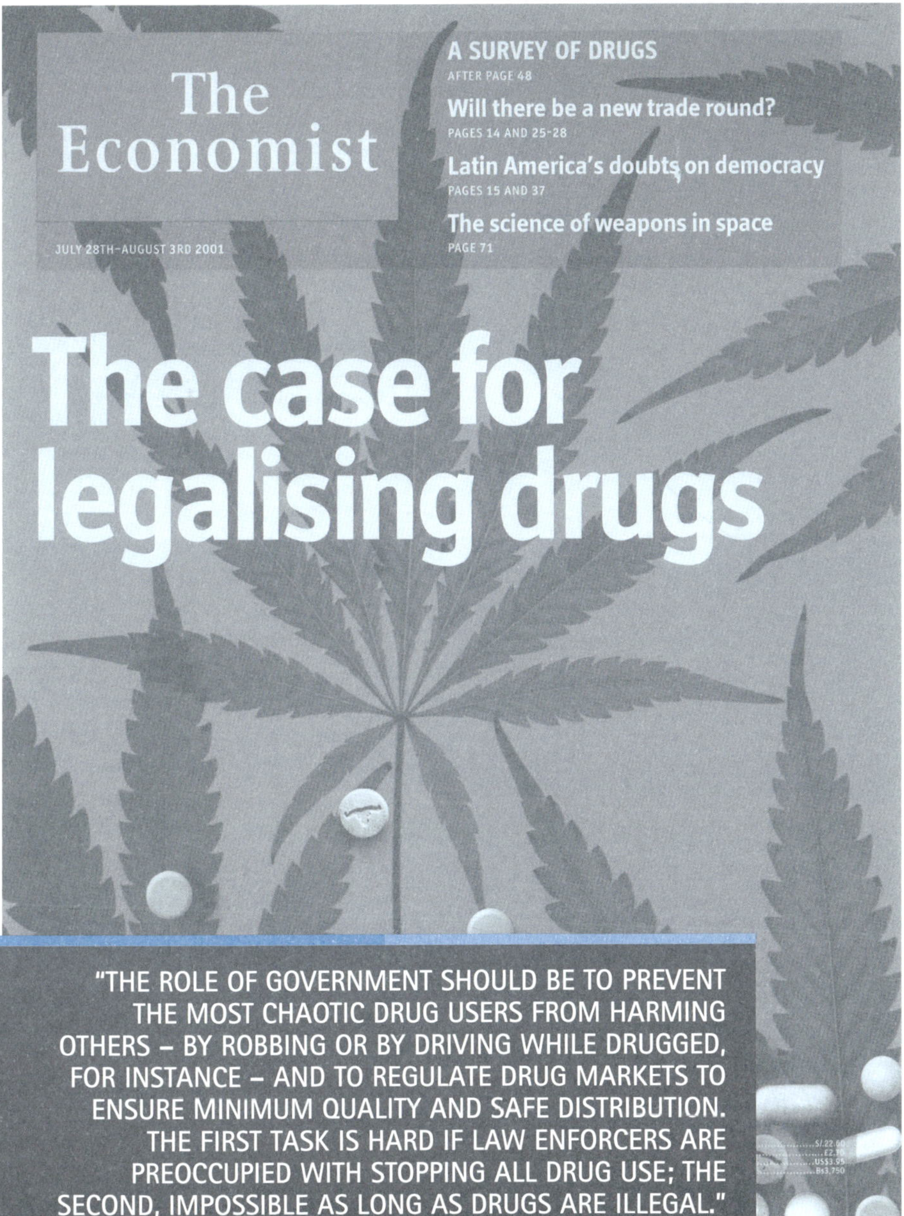

"THE ROLE OF GOVERNMENT SHOULD BE TO PREVENT THE MOST CHAOTIC DRUG USERS FROM HARMING OTHERS – BY ROBBING OR BY DRIVING WHILE DRUGGED, FOR INSTANCE – AND TO REGULATE DRUG MARKETS TO ENSURE MINIMUM QUALITY AND SAFE DISTRIBUTION. THE FIRST TASK IS HARD IF LAW ENFORCERS ARE PREOCCUPIED WITH STOPPING ALL DRUG USE; THE SECOND, IMPOSSIBLE AS LONG AS DRUGS ARE ILLEGAL."

THE ECONOMIST
EDITORIAL. FROM ISSUE ENTITLED: 'TIME TO LEGALISE ALL DRUGS' 28.06.01

5. CONCERNS ABOUT MOVES TOWARDS LEGALLY REGULATED MARKETS

THIS SECTION OF THE GUIDE PROVIDES THE BASIC ANALYSIS YOU WILL NEED TO RESPOND TO THE MOST COMMONLY RAISED CONCERNS ABOUT LEGALISATION AND REGULATION.

MANY OF THESE CONCERNS ARE STRESSED REPEATEDLY BY THOSE WHO SEEK TO MAINTAIN PROHIBITION AND UNDERMINE THE REFORM MOVEMENT. SO WHILST IT IS IMPORTANT TO RESPECT AND RESPOND SENSIBLY TO LEGITIMATE CONCERNS AS A WAY OF FINDING COMMON GROUND, YOU MAY ALSO HAVE TO BATTLE AGAINST CYNICAL ATTEMPTS TO DISCREDIT YOU FROM THOSE INTENT ON MAINTAINING THE FAULT LINES IN THE DEBATE. CONSIDER THE MOTIVATIONS OF THOSE WHO RAISE THESE CONCERNS, AND BE PARTICULARLY WARY – AND, WHEN NECESSARY, MERCILESS – WHEN IT IS A POLITICIAN DEFENDING A PARTY LINE OR USING A SMOKESCREEN TO PROTECT THE STATUS QUO FROM SCRUTINY.

1. WILL PREVALENCE OF USE RISE?

Prohibitionists maintain at least a rhetorical commitment to the elimination of drugs from society and it is in this context that measurements of prevalence of use have assumed huge importance in the policy reform debate. For opponents of reform, the spectre of rising use following any moves toward legally regulated production and supply is the key argument which comes up again and again. Unfortunately the response to it, whilst coherent, is a tricky one to boil down into a simple sound bite, essentially because the point being made is 'well, it's a lot more complicated than that' - which, as it happens, is probably your best starting point.

This is a tricky issue and may require a detailed response (offered below), but if you absolutely have to be concise, the basic points of the response are that:

- The impact of policy and law on levels of use is marginal (in some cases even contributing to increases) - cultural and socio-economic variables are far more important. Prohibition has demonstrably failed to prevent the dramatic rise in drug use and drug harms over the past four decades.

- Drug use may both rise and fall post prohibition - there will be a range of factors at play, and we will certainly see different impacts with different drugs, different populations of users and different locations

- What is absolutely certain is that overall harm associated with drugs will fall - the risks associated with drug use will decrease sharply and society will be far better placed to address problematic drug use, and its underlying causes

- Reducing drug related harm is more important than the futile pursuit of a drug free society

The UK national drugs strategy states that "... we will prevent young people from using drugs by maintaining prohibition which deters use...". Similarly The Home Office states that "Drugs are controlled because of their harm potential and the law and its sanctions help to limit experimentation". This understanding is reflected in much of the popular political and media opposition to reforms with frequent references, most recently witnessed during the cannabis reclassification debate, to 'giving the green light to drug use' or 'sending out the wrong message'. As so often in the drugs debate, these simple arguments conceal more complex and important ones and the apparent fault line here is not nearly as clear cut as it may initially seem:

- The idea that drug use will rise post-prohibition is built on guesswork and the very

> "RISK FACTORS -PARTICULARLY RELATING TO DEPRIVATION -ARE THE PRIME DETERMINANT OF INITIATION INTO PROBLEMATIC DRUG USE; PRICE AND AVAILABILITY PLAY A SECONDARY ROLE"
>
> "THERE IS NO CAUSAL RELATIONSHIP BETWEEN AVAILABILITY AND INCIDENCE; INDEED, PRICES AND INCIDENCE OFTEN FALL OR RISE AT THE SAME TIME"
>
> NO. 10 STRATEGY UNIT DRUGS PROJECT
>
> PHASE 2 REPORT: "DIAGNOSIS AND RECOMMENDATIONS"2003

flimsy premise that prohibition is an effective deterrent to use. Research into drug taking motivations, specifically why people choose not to take drugs, and the extent of any deterrent effect from law enforcement, is extremely scant. The Home Office has never undertaken or presented any substantial evidence in support of the alleged deterrent effect that is at the heart of UK drug policy - even when it has been specifically and repeatedly challenged on this issue by various parliamentary select committees. From the little we do have, it appears the extent and impact of enforcement related deterrence is at best marginal, and will vary greatly between different drugs and drug using groups. (see also: - Myths about prohibition: the criminal justice system is an effective deterrent p.25).

- In particular there is no evidence to demonstrate a deterrent effect amongst problematic or dependent users of heroin and cocaine, the Government's stated primary focus of its drug policy efforts.

- There are a large number of variables that affect drug-taking decisions other than enforcement related deterrence. These significantly include socioeconomic variables, fashion, culture and music, advertising, availability, price and perception of risk. Post-prohibition there will be effects that may increase use (removal of enforcement deterrence, lower price, easier availability, better quality), as well as effects that may lower use (removal of 'underground glamour', more medicalisation of addicts, removal of dealers targeting new users, increased investment in treatment, education and social regeneration). The net effect of these conflicting pressures is unclear and will vary significantly between different drugs and different drug using populations.

"IN THE FACE OF ALL THE EVIDENCE, THOROUGH RESEARCH INTO THE POSSIBILITY OF LEGALISATION IS THE ONLY INTELLIGENT THING TO DO."

PROFESSOR SHEILA BIRD
PRINCIPAL STATISTICIAN AT THE MEDICAL RESEARCH COUNCIL BIOSTATISTICS UNIT.
CAMBRIDGE EVENING NEWS MARCH 2006

- Headline figures of reported use give no indication of the intensity or frequency of use, and specifically do not measure problematic use or levels of harm associated with use. A rise in prevalence does not necessarily equate to a rise in overall harm, and could in theory coincide with a fall in the prevalence of problematic use and overall harm.

- A report commissioned by Tony Blair from the Number 10 Strategy Unit concluded that "There is no causal relationship between drug availability and incidence [of use] " and "Supply-side interventions have a limited role to play in reducing harm - initiation into problematic drug use is not driven by changes in availability or price" [12].

It is also important to acknowledge how the nature of drug use would change under a legally regulated system that we believe would mean that, even if there were an increase in use, there would be a decrease in overall harm:

- Drugs would be safer, being of known and guaranteed strength and purity and having health and safety information, warnings and guidance on packaging or available at point of sale.

- Prohibition has pushed users towards ever

more concentrated and profitable forms of certain drugs (from opium to heroin, and from coca leaf to coca drinks to cocaine to crack). A post prohibition era is likely to witness a shift back towards safer, less concentrated options. By way of example, following the end of alcohol prohibition in the US consumption patterns moved away from spirits back to beers and wines (see 'talking about .....Alcohol and Tobacco? p.37 and 'Talking about .....crack? p.41)

Prevalence of use is only one of a number of health indicators (and not an especially useful one) and health is only one of a number of policy areas that need to be evaluated.

Policy should seek to manage drug use so as to minimise the harm drugs cause, both to drug users and the wider community. This requires that we redefine 'the drug problem' as more than just 'people use drugs'. Measuring the effectiveness of drug policy requires a far broader range of indicators that include public health, crime, civil rights, community safety and international development and conflict.

"THE KING COUNTY BAR ASSOCIATION HAS CONCLUDED... THAT THE ESTABLISHMENT OF A NEW LEGAL FRAMEWORK OF STATE-LEVEL REGULATORY CONTROL OVER PSYCHOACTIVE SUBSTANCES, INTENDED TO RENDER THE ILLEGAL MARKETS FOR SUCH SUBSTANCES UNPROFITABLE, TO RESTRICT ACCESS TO PSYCHOACTIVE SUBSTANCES BY YOUNG PERSONS AND TO PROVIDE PROMPT HEALTH CARE AND ESSENTIAL SERVICES TO PERSONS SUFFERING FROM CHEMICAL DEPENDENCY AND ADDICTION, WILL BETTER SERVE THE OBJECTIVES OF REDUCING CRIME, IMPROVING PUBLIC ORDER, ENHANCING PUBLIC HEALTH, PROTECTING CHILDREN AND WISELY USING SCARCE PUBLIC RESOURCES, THAN CURRENT DRUG POLICIES".

KING COUNTY BAR ASSOCIATION,
'EFFECTIVE DRUG CONTROL: TOWARD A NEW LEGAL FRAMEWORK' 2005

2. VULNERABLE GROUPS: WHAT ABOUT THE KIDS?

After 'drug use would go up', the next most frequently voiced concern about the moves towards legally regulated drugs is best summarised as 'but what about the kids?'. For parents and carers in particular it is entirely understandable that there are real fears about the impact of drug law reform on the most vulnerable in society, children and young people, as well as people with mental health problems, the homeless and other socially excluded groups.

These fears continue to be stoked up by the defenders of prohibition in vociferous and populist appeals to emotions over evidence. Heart-rending tales of tragic and wasted youth are used by politicians and prohibitionists as 'anecdata', a rhetorical ploy to avoid substantive discussion of the overwhelmingly negative effects of prohibition - from Afghanistan through Iran to Brixton, and Colombia through the Caribbean to Moss Side. Many career politicians and policy-makers are well aware that 'what about the kids?' is a line that can be exploited to deflect the focus of the debate away from areas where they may be exposed.

KEY POINTS TO MAKE WHEN THIS ISSUE ARISES:

- The reality is that under the current regime illegal drugs remain easily available to most young people and a significant minority have used one or more. Regulation cannot eliminate such use, any more than it can with tobacco and alcohol, but controlled availability will create a significantly improved environment for reducing harm, and longer term reductions in demand. One of the key benefits of regulation is that it allows appropriate controls to be put in place over price and availability (location, times of opening and age restrictions) as well as controls over advertising and promotion. It is precisely because drugs pose risks that they need to be appropriately regulated, especially for young people.

- legally regulated and controlled drug markets will offer a far greater level of protection to vulnerable groups than the chaotic, unregulated and often violent illegal markets we have today

- Prohibition directly endangers and harms young people; they are the most frequent victims of drug motivated street crime and violence and they carry the increased burden of risk from using illegal drugs of unknown strength and purity

- The greatest threat from drugs to the health of the young still comes, by a substantial margin, from tobacco and alcohol. Legal regulation will facilitate a more balanced, consistent and believable health message on all drugs

- A criminal record (even for a minor drug offence) can have a devastating effect on already vulnerable individuals, fostering social exclusion. A criminal record puts significant restrictions on employment, travel, personal finance, and housing. For many young people it is a greater threat to their health and well-being than occasional drug use, particularly if it involves the trauma of imprisonment

- Young people are not stupid. Policies that they rightly perceive to be failing, hypocritical, unfair, persecuting, mean and pointless can only undermine respect for the law, the police and authority in general. If we want to reach out to young people and other vulnerable or socially excluded groups, in order to offer help and encourage responsible lifestyle choices, then declaring a war against them is not the way to do it. Removing the spectre of criminality would make drug services and information far more attractive and accessible for those most in need but hardest to reach.

(see also – 'minimising harm to the young and vulnerable' p.23)

> **"SO LONG AS LARGE SUMS OF MONEY ARE INVOLVED – AND THEY ARE BOUND TO BE IF DRUGS ARE ILLEGAL – IT IS LITERALLY IMPOSSIBLE TO STOP THE TRAFFIC, OR EVEN TO MAKE A SERIOUS REDUCTION IN ITS SCOPE."**
>
> MILTON FRIEDMAN,
> NOBEL PRIZE WINNER (ECONOMICS)
> TYRANNY OF THE STATUS QUO 1984

3. WILL PROFIT MOTIVATED MULTINATIONALS TAKE OVER CONTROL FROM THE CARTELS?

There is a legitimate concern that legal drug markets could eventually be controlled by profit-motivated corporations interested in aggressively marketing and promoting drugs and drug use. The pharmaceutical industry is already the focus of considerable criticism for some of its ethical, business and marketing practices. Similarly, sections of the alcohol and (particularly) tobacco industries have been guilty of unethical conduct, putting profits before concerns for public health with aggressive youth-oriented marketing through, for example, sport and music sponsorship. However, for all the criticisms of commercial companies, they are infinitely preferable to the alternative of international organised criminal networks. To illustrate this point it should be noted that unlike gangsters the commercial companies:

- pay tax
- are subject to external scrutiny in the form of independent auditors, trade and financial regulatory bodies, unions and consumer groups
- are answerable to the law and are legally liable for their actions
- are not armed and do not use violence in their daily business dealings
- can be controlled and regulated as deemed appropriate by democratically elected governments

"AND IF WE WANT TO HELP SUSTAINABLE ECONOMIC DEVELOPMENT IN THE DRUG-RIDDEN STATES SUCH AS COLOMBIA AND AFGHANISTAN, WE SHOULD ALMOST CERTAINLY LIBERALISE DRUGS USE IN OUR SOCIETIES, COMBATING ABUSE VIA EDUCATION, NOT PROHIBITION, RATHER THAN LAUNCHING UNWINNABLE 'WARS ON DRUGS' WHICH SIMPLY CRIMINALISE WHOLE SOCIETIES."

ADAIR TURNER
CHAIRMAN OF THE UK PENSIONS COMMISSION AND THE UK LOW PAY COMMISSION, TRUSTEE OF WWF, FORMER DIRECTOR OF THE CBI. SPEECH TO THE WWF 06.11.03

Emerging legal drug markets offer a blank slate, a rare opportunity for us to establish the optimum legal regulatory framework that functions in the public's best interests. If, for example, commercial companies are deemed unsuitable, then production or supply of certain more dangerous drugs could become an entirely state run enterprise. When bookies were legalised the Tote was (and remains) a state-run business, with private companies entering the market at a later stage.

Existing production and supply models for currently legal drugs, with some modification, will be appropriate for most drugs. Lessons learnt from problems with existing legislation for legal drugs are already informing sweeping reforms such as bans on tobacco advertising and smoking in public buildings (see: 'talking about....alcohol and tobacco' p.37). These lessons will also help us develop more effective regulation for drugs in the post-prohibition era, avoiding the mistakes of the past.

"IF THERE IS ANY SINGLE LESSON FROM THE EXPERIENCE OF THE LAST 30 YEARS, IT IS THAT POLICIES BASED WHOLLY OR MAINLY ON ENFORCEMENT ARE DESTINED TO FAIL."

"HARM REDUCTION RATHER THAN RETRIBUTION SHOULD BE THE PRIMARY FOCUS OF POLICY TOWARDS USERS OF ILLEGAL DRUGS. WE ARE GLAD TO NOTE THAT THE GOVERNMENT IS MAKING THE FIRST TENTATIVE STEPS IN THAT DIRECTION. WE BELIEVE IT SHOULD GO FURTHER"

HOME AFFAIRS SELECT COMMITTEE
REPORT 'THE GOVERNMENT'S DRUG POLICY: IS IT WORKING?' 09.05.02

4. MORALS AND MESSAGES

As discussed earlier (p.52) the morality of drug use, legal or illegal, is best avoided as a topic. It is a polarising issue, and also a pointless one, as policy simply has to deal with the reality - that a majority of people use drugs of one form or another. If the topic does arise, tackle it sensitively. Always point out that personal moral choices are different from moral policy making, which should always seek to minimise harms for individuals and society. Do not surrender the moral high ground to advocates of counterproductive policies that have created immense harm and suffering.

The Home Office argues that 'Drugs are controlled because of their harm potential and the law and its sanctions help to limit experimentation'. Yet, as already discussed, we do not prohibit by law the possession of high-powered motorcycles, rock climbing, casual sex without condoms, high fat junk foods, alcohol, tobacco, or any number of other activities and consumables that involve risk to the user, with equivalent or higher 'harm potential' than illegal drug use. When the Government wishes to send messages encouraging sensible, healthy or safer lifestyle choices - for everything other than illegal drugs - it uses public education via a range of institutions and media.

Drug policy is unique in using the criminal justice system and the threat of arrest, criminality and imprisonment as a primary educational tool. It is not the job of the criminal justice system to send messages on public health or private morality, and when it has attempted to do so it has been singularly ineffective. There is nothing moral in pursuing a policy that has created so much crime, violence and conflict, that criminalises and marginalises the most needy and vulnerable members of our society, and that maximises the risks associated with drug use. Transform believes that policy should seek to minimise the harm drugs cause to users and the wider community, rather than seek to enforce a personal moral position by increasing harm to others.

5. A LEAP IN THE DARK?

It is often suggested that legalisation and regulation would be a dangerous gamble with the health and well-being of the public, and that there is no evidence to support such a radical move (this was the main argument against legalisation put forward by the Home Affairs Select Committee Inquiry in 2002[19]). Whilst it is true that no country has yet legalised and regulated any of the drugs covered under the UN conventions, it is wrong to suggest that there is no evidence to support reform arguments. A significant body of evidence in support of drug policy and law reform can be assembled from a range of sources:

- Currently legal drugs. Most obviously there is evidence from the effective, if imperfect, functioning of regulatory models for currently legal drugs, primarily alcohol and tobacco. These are toxic and highly addictive drugs that are associated with significant health and social harms. However, their legal regulation means the government can intervene in areas such as price and availability and they are not associated with most of the social harms created by prohibition regards production (see: 'talking about...alcohol and tobacco' p.37).

- The end of alcohol prohibition. The problems created by alcohol prohibition closely echo those of modern drug prohibition, and the benefits of its repeal are well documented.

- Heroin prescribing. The prescription model for drug supply has a significant body of evidence in its support[20]. Large scale heroin prescription projects have been adopted in countries across Western Europe including Holland, Germany, and Switzerland with impressive results on indicators for crime, health and social nuisance. Evidence also comes from the UK which pioneered heroin prescribing from the 1920s, only to see it heavily restricted from the 70s onwards. It should be noted that the prescribing model still functions in the UK, with certain individuals prescribed maintenance heroin in injectable form. The numbers receiving prescriptions is small, around 300, but plans have been announced by the (former) Home Secretary to expand this number to around 2000. In this sense, legal control and regulation of the most dangerous drug is already in operation.

- The de-facto decriminalisation of personal possession of drugs has taken place in numerous countries, most commonly for cannabis, but in some cases, - including Portugal, Spain, Italy, Western Australia and Russia - the change encompasses all drugs.

- The Dutch cannabis experiment. In Holland, not only has possession of cannabis been decriminalised, but sales from shops have been tolerated and licensed since 1976. Whilst it technically remains illegal, the pragmatic Dutch model has come closest to showing how a legal cannabis market can operate effectively. The policy, in contrast to disparaging claims made by prohibitionist detractors, has been effective and enjoys broad public and official support. It is useful to point out that since these moves Holland has historically had lower levels of cannabis use than either the US or UK (although all have risen).

- Legalisation and regulation of gambling and prostitution. Although these are activities rather than products they illustrate how violence, criminal markets and other problems associated with high demand for illegal activities can be minimised through legal regulation.

By contrast, the evidence is both extensive and conclusive that prohibition has failed, both in the UK and internationally. Prohibition itself had no evidence base when it was devised and implemented. It could itself be described as a huge leap in the dark, gambling with the health and well-being of the public, and demonstrably failing on its own terms. By contrast, the moves to regulated markets have a wealth of evidence to show how they would work and the benefits they would bring. There is clearly more work to be done: we need assessments, pilot studies and other research designed to develop and implement new policy (a veritable army of civil servants will be freed up as the enforcement approach is wound down). However, from what we already know it is clear that moves towards legal regulation are far from a leap in the dark.

6. HOW DO WE GET THERE?

Even once people have understood the reform position and support it in principle, doubts may remain about the feasibility of making progress, given the wider political climate, public opinion and the numerous domestic and international institutional hurdles.

It is important to stress that change will come in increments over a number of years and a new post-prohibition world will not spring into being overnight. Already this process is underway on many levels:

- Personal use of drugs is widely (de facto) decriminalised in much of Western Europe, Russia, and regions of Canada, Australia and South America.

- Supervised injecting rooms (and drug smoking rooms) have been established in Vancouver, Sydney, and across Europe.

- Heroin and other drugs, including stimulants, are available through medical prescription, to long term problem users in a number of countries including the UK, Canada, Australia, Switzerland and Germany.

- Cannabis cultivation is decriminalised in some countries/regions and licensed sales are allowed in Holland.

- There is a global trend away from harsh, costly and ineffective enforcement, towards a greater emphasis on treatment, harm reduction and approaching problem drug use primarily as a public health issue.

These changes are chipping away at the monolith of prohibition in many different places. At one end, we can expect an expansion of medical maintenance prescribing of opiates, and some stimulants (possibly including cocaine); at the other end, moves towards the decriminalisation and eventual legalisation and regulation of cannabis and other comparatively low risk drugs (simultaneously we are witnessing tightening of regulation of alcohol and tobacco). Different countries will move at different paces and information from those experiences will feed into the body of knowledge about what works best for different drugs in different environments.

Transform has produced a history of prohibition time line[1] – that looks into the future to map out these how these changes may develop over the coming 10-15 years.

7. DON'T THE UN TREATIES MEAN REFORM IS IMPOSSIBLE?

The UN drugs treaties present a significant but by no means insurmountable hurdle. They were formulated in a long distant era (some of the 1961 convention was drafted in the 1940s, when

"WE RECOMMEND THAT THE GOVERNMENT INITIATES A DISCUSSION WITHIN THE COMMISSION ON NARCOTIC DRUGS OF ALTERNATIVE WAYS – INCLUDING THE POSSIBILITY OF LEGALISATION AND REGULATION – TO TACKLE THE GLOBAL DRUGS DILEMMA."

HOME AFFAIRS SELECT COMMITTEE
REPORT 'THE GOVERNMENT'S DRUG POLICY: IS IT WORKING?' 09.05.02

Al Capone was still alive) when the nature of the drug problem was unrecognisably different from the situation today. They are laws from the distant past that have dramatically failed in their stated goal of reducing drug availability and harms, and are too rigidly drawn to adapt to our present-day needs.

Mechanisms do exist to redraft and change the treaties - but these are riddled with political and institutional problems[21]. Unilateral withdrawal or denunciation presents significant political costs to individual states but may be facilitated by three factors in the coming years.

1. There is a coalition of countries that are deeply and increasingly unhappy with the conventions, and will sooner or later present their objections under a united front.

2. The strength of the treaties is diminishing with each year, as they consistently fail to deliver what they set out to. They are withering on the vine as more and more countries move away from the letter and spirit of the laws they enshrine and become increasingly reluctant to fund their expensive and failed programmes.

3. There is increasing conflict between the UN drug agencies that dogmatically adhere to an outdated prohibitionist paradigm, and other UN agencies including the WHO, the UNHCR, and UNAIDS, who increasingly subscribe to more progressive and pragmatic human rights, harm reduction and public health principles.

THE KEY POINTS HERE ARE:

- UK and other Governments need to show leadership, embrace modernity and challenge outdated and ineffectual legislation in whatever arena it arises.

- There is a great deal that can be done in the short term within the treaties that is avoided by governments who misleadingly deploy the treaties as an excuse for inaction. There is nothing to stop us, for example, from setting up supervised injecting rooms, prescribing drugs to problematic users, shifting enforcement priorities towards de facto decriminalisation of certain offences, or moving from criminal to civil penalties for certain offences.

- UN treaties are not, despite the protestations of some prohibitionists, written in stone. They can be and frequently are redrafted where the political will exists, and there are other exit options that can be pursued unilaterally or as part of a coalition of progressive states.

Transform has outlined the steps by which this process could occur in its history of prohibition time line.[1]

8. WHERE WILL ALL THE CRIMINALS GO?

This concern has cropped up more and more recently, which we take to be a sign that the other more substantive concerns are being adequately responded to. It does have some legitimacy: if the most lucrative source of illegal income is denied to organised criminals, what will they all do?

The Association of Chief Police Officers, in arguments to the Home Affairs Select Committee[19] suggested it was absurd to think legalisation would cause drug gangs to just 'fade into the night'. Obviously it is ridiculous to imagine they will all 'go straight' and get jobs in McDonalds, or selling flowers, but it is equally absurd to suggest they will all embark on some previously unimagined crime spree. Clearly the impacts will differ at the various levels of the criminal infrastructure and, since reforms will be phased over a number of years and not happen overnight, criminal drug infrastructures will experience a twilight period of diminishing profit opportunities.

> "MANY OFFICERS BELIEVE THE 33-YEAR-OLD ACT IS NOT ONLY OUTDATED, BUT DANGEROUS AND HARMFUL, BOTH TO ADDICTS AND TO RECREATIONAL DRUG USERS, AS IT FOCUSES ON LOCKING UP SMALL-TIME OFFENDERS WHILST INADVERTENTLY GRANTING THE MONOPOLY OF DRUG SUPPLY TO HIGH-RANKING CRIMINALS."
>
> MORRIE FLOWERS,
> CHAIRMAN OF THE SCOTTISH POLICE FEDERATION
> THE SCOTSMAN 13.04.06

Undoubtedly some criminals will seek out new areas of illegal activity and it is realistic to expect that there may be increases in some areas, such as cyber-crime, extortion or other illicit trades (counterfeit goods etc.). However, crime is to a large extent a function of opportunity, and it is impossible to imagine that there is enough criminal opportunity to absorb the manpower currently operating an illicit drugs market with a turnover somewhere in the region of £300 billion pounds a year globally, or over £6 billion a year in the UK alone[22]. Even if there is some diversion into other criminal activity, the big picture will undoubtedly show a significant net fall in overall criminal activity. Getting rid of illegal drug markets is about reducing opportunities for crime.

This concern is a curious one because it seems, when considered closely, to be advocating prohibition as a way of maintaining illegal drug empires so that organised criminals don't have to change jobs. By contrast, from our perspective the argument is about removing the largest criminal opportunity on earth, not just from existing criminals but, significantly, from future generations of criminals. Ending prohibition holds the prospect of diverting millions of potential young drug producers, traffickers, and dealers from a life of crime.

9. WHEN BAD THINGS HAPPEN

Negative stories about illegal drugs, involving crime, violence or death, always bring the drug policy debate into the spotlight, and invariably in the worst possible way: emotive and sensationalised by 'shock' tabloid headlines and ripe for political exploitation. Notorious examples include the high profile deaths of Leah Betts in

1995 following ecstasy use (although the cause of death has subsequently been associated with acute water intoxication), and Rachel Whitear who died of a heroin overdose in 2000. More recently we have seen a spate of high-profile reporting of violent crimes associated with mentally ill individuals who also used various legal and illegal drugs – with the illegal drugs, rather than any of the other factors, being directly blamed for the incident in shock terms ('CANNABIS CRAZED AXE MURDERER').

In media reporting, the 'if it bleeds - it leads' ethos means that such events tend to dominate the debate around responses to drugs in society. This promotes a one dimensional debate and a repetitive insistence that drugs are an 'evil' we must fight against, whilst doing nothing to promote the responses that might make such tragedies less likely. What is the best way to respond?

- Acknowledge the tragedy and try to move the discussion on to ways in which such events might be avoided in the future. You can point out that knee-jerk responses to such events and the 'moral panics' they provoke do not have a history of creating effective policy.

- Not only have such tragedies occurred under prohibition with increasing frequency, but illegal markets make such events more likely. Prohibition actively increases risks associated with drug use and also directly fuels crime and violence. All these tragedies have occurred under prohibition, so how can prohibition be the answer?

- Directing resources into counter-productive enforcement diverts funding from precisely the sort of public health interventions (education, prevention, treatment etc.) that may reduce the incidence of such tragedies.

"LAW ENFORCEMENT AGAINST PROHIBITION IS MADE UP OF [OVER 5000] CURRENT AND FORMER MEMBERS OF LAW ENFORCEMENT WHO BELIEVE THE EXISTING DRUG POLICIES HAVE FAILED IN THEIR INTENDED GOALS OF ADDRESSING THE PROBLEMS OF CRIME, DRUG ABUSE, ADDICTION, JUVENILE DRUG USE, STOPPING THE FLOW OF ILLEGAL DRUGS INTO THIS COUNTRY AND THE INTERNAL SALE AND USE OF ILLEGAL DRUGS. BY FIGHTING A WAR ON DRUGS THE GOVERNMENT HAS INCREASED THE PROBLEMS OF SOCIETY AND MADE THEM FAR WORSE. A SYSTEM OF REGULATION RATHER THAN PROHIBITION IS A LESS HARMFUL, MORE ETHICAL AND A MORE EFFECTIVE PUBLIC POLICY.

"THE MISSION OF LEAP IS TO REDUCE THE MULTITUDE OF UNINTENDED HARMFUL CONSEQUENCES RESULTING FROM FIGHTING THE WAR ON DRUGS AND TO LESSEN THE INCIDENCE OF DEATH, DISEASE, CRIME, AND ADDICTION BY ULTIMATELY ENDING DRUG PROHIBITION."

QUOTE FROM THE MISSION STATEMENT OF LAW ENFORCEMENT AGAINST PROHIBITION.

7. FURTHER RESOURCES

TO BECOME AN UNASSAILABLE ADVOCATE FOR DRUG POLICY REFORM YOU WILL NEED TO HAVE THE BEST POSSIBLE FACTS, ANALYSIS AND ARGUMENT AT YOUR FINGERTIPS. THIS GUIDE CAN POINT YOU IN THE RIGHT DIRECTION BUT YOU WILL NEED TO MAKE SURE YOU HAVE DONE THE APPROPRIATE RESEARCH FOR YOU CHOSEN TOPIC AND AUDIENCE.

The Transform website www.tdpf.org.uk is the best place to start. There you can find:

- An extensive range of briefings on specific topics
- Transform's fact research guide – providing headline statistics, guides to sources of information on key topics and a review of the quality of data available on each
- The Transform quote archive – supporters of reform from politics and public life
- Links to key reports from Parliament and Whitehall, NGO and academic sources
- Media articles and news reports
- Categorised links to independent and Government organisations and information sources in the UK and around the world
- Links to key Parliamentary activity and debate

YOU CAN ALSO CONTACT TRANSFORM DIRECTLY FOR HELP WITH SPECIFIC QUERIES. PLEASE EMAIL INFO@TDPF.ORG.UK OR CALL THE TRANSFORM OFFICE ON 0117 941 5810

KEY REPORTS ON POLICY ALTERNATIVES TO PROHIBITION

Note: All of the reports listed below are freely available online and are linked here: www.tdpf.org.uk/Policy_KeyReports

BRITISH COLOMBIA HEALTH OFFICERS COUNCIL 'A PUBLIC HEALTH APPROACH TO DRUG CONTROL' (2005)

This report was produced by an independent group of public health officials in British Colombia, Canada, and is a detailed consideration of regulatory options for currently illegal drugs. Thoughtful, detailed and logical analysis - some of the clearest objective thinking ever done on the subject.

THE KING COUNTY BAR ASSOCIATION: 'EFFECTIVE DRUG CONTROL: TOWARD A NEW LEGAL FRAMEWORK' (2005)

This report comes from the drug policy project of the Kings County (Seattle) Bar Association. A detailed discussion of frameworks for drug regulation from a legal rather than public heath perspective. A comprehensive review of regulatory options and wider policy considerations.

TRANSFORM DRUG POLICY FOUNDATION "AFTER THE WAR ON DRUGS - OPTIONS FOR CONTROL" (2004)

Transform's report examines the key themes in the drug policy reform debate, detailing how legal regulation of drug markets will operate, and providing a roadmap for reform.

COMING SOON – Transform is currently working in conjunction with the HOBC and KCBA to produce the definitive guide to drug policy and law reform, combining and developing the work of the three reports detailed above. 'After the War on Drugs - A Blueprint for Change' is due for publication in Spring 2008

REVIEWS OF UK DRUG POLICY

REPORT OF THE INDEPENDENT INQUIRY INTO THE MISUSE OF DRUGS ACT 1971 POLICE FOUNDATION (2000).

(ALSO KNOWN AS 'THE RUNCIMAN REPORT' AFTER THE INQUIRY CHAIR DAME RUTH RUNCIMAN)

This inquiry was set up in August 1997 by the independent charity the Police Foundation (not to be confused with the Police Federation) to review the effectiveness of the Misuse of Drugs Act 1971. It made a detailed analysis of current policy failings and offered recommendations for a number of practical reforms, including the reclassification of cannabis, ecstasy and LSD, and focusing spending on health rather than punitive enforcement. It did not examine the possibility of decriminalisation or legalisation/regulation in any detail, but still provides a useful factual and historical analysis of drug policy in the UK, and sets the scene for the Home Affairs Select Committee report which followed it.

HOME AFFAIRS SELECT COMMITTEE: THE GOVERNMENT'S DRUG POLICY: IS IT WORKING? (2002)

An in-depth critique of UK policy and the first detailed parliamentary consideration of decriminalisation and legalisation since the

1971 Misuse of Drugs Act entered the statute books. The range of expert witness evidence taken and the scope and detail of the report was unprecedented. It again provides a useful factual and historical summary of the drug phenomenon in the UK and offers a spectrum of progressive responses. Whilst stopping short of calling for substantive law reform its final recommendation was "that the Government initiates a discussion within the Commission on narcotic drugs of alternative ways - including the possibility of legalsiation and regulation - to tackle the global drugs dilemma."

THE PRIME MINSTER'S NO 10 STRATEGY UNIT REPORT: UNDERSTANDING THE ISSUES (2003)

The Prime Minister's Strategy Unit produced a detailed economic and social analysis of International and domestic drug policy. This is an extremely useful document: firstly because of its structured, well referenced and clearly presented factual content (designed for ministerial consumption), and secondly because of its provenance, commissioned by and presented to the Prime Minister, having been researched and drafted by some of the UK's top policy thinkers. Its analysis showed with crystal clarity how supply-side enforcement interventions are ineffective and indeed actively counterproductive - presumably why the Government tried unsuccessfully to prevent its publication (it was leaked to the Guardian).

THE SCIENCE AND TECHNOLOGY SELECT COMMITTEE REPORT ON DRUG CLASSIFICATION 'MAKING A HASH OF IT' (2006)

This report put the ABC drug classification system and the scientific basis of drug policy generally under some close and overdue scientific scrutiny. There is some critique of the institutions involved, but more useful is the detailed analysis of the unscientific way in which drug policy has been devised and implemented - considering the lack of evidence for a deterrent effect for example. Very useful and informative review from a scientific perspective rather than an overtly political one.

RSA COMMISSION ON ILLEGAL DRUGS, COMMUNITIES AND PUBLIC POLICY (2007)

Described as an 'Unofficial Royal Commission' the RSA (Royal Society for the Encouragement Arts Manufactures and Commerce) Commission on Illegal Drugs, Communities and Public Policy report was set up to take a fresh look at the drug policy and try to untangle the complex knot of issues commonly referred to as 'the drugs problem'. A detailed and forward thinking analysis whose otherwise commendable recommendations hint at, but stop just shy of, calls for legalisation and regulation.

JUST THE FACTS

TRANSFORM'S FACT RESEARCH GUIDE is a new addition to the Transform website, offering a critical guide to available information on key topics in the drugs debate, both official and independent.
www.tdpf.org.uk/Policy_FactResearchGuide.htm

DRUGSCOPE INFORMATION SERVICES

Drugscope is an independent umbrella group providing information services to over 900 member organisations in the drugs field. It provides an unrivalled range of useful information services based around its unique and extensive drug literature library.
www.drugscope.co.uk

GOVERNMENT INFORMATION SERVICES

Various government and parliamentary agencies

produce statistical bulletins, reports and analysis. Good places to start are:

The www.drugs.gov website – in theory a portal for most relevant Government reports and data, although in practice it can be quite difficult to pin down what you are really after as the site content reflects a political need to present the drug strategy in a positive light. If, for example you wanted to know whether drugs had become less available over the past 10 years (a key target of the drug strategy) the publications section under 'drug supply' will provide little illumination. However, there is some very useful content here, including publications by the Advisory Council on the Misuse of Drugs which are of consistently high quality.

Often more useful is the Home Office research development statistics drugs page – www.homeoffice.gov.uk/rds/ which lists all published Home Office statistical bulletins, reports and analysis. It is more statistically heavy than the more public face of the drugs.gov site and will require considerably more digging and interpretation but, if you have the patience, it is the best source of un-spun official Home Office data and research.

THE RHETORIC

Transform's published articles web page contains a collection of our various writings and commentary printed in national media and specialised publications, including a collection of our published letters.
www.tdpf.org.uk/MediaNews_TransformInTheMedia

Transform has an extensive collection of quotes from high profile public figures in support of drug law reform. The quote archive is divided into the following sections; Politics, Opinion Formers, Criminal Justice, Celebrities/Public Figures, NGOs and Statutory sector, and Religious Leaders. This collection will provide inspiration, guidance on language and presentation for different audiences, as well as reassurance that you, as a reformer, are in very distinguished company.
www.tdpf.org.uk/MediaNews_Reform_supporters

Transform has a web page listing recent debates on drug policy issues in The House of Commons and The House of Lords. There are many eloquent and passionate reformers in both Houses and the links provided provide a useful lesson on how to debate this issue in the political arena, as well as the familiar rhetorical devices used by the defenders of prohibition. You can also use the excellent website www.theyworkforyou.com to do key word searches of the all recent parliamentary activity, including debate and parliamentary questions.
www.tdpf.org.uk/Parliament_Debates

YOU CAN LEARN A LOT FROM THE NUMEROUS PRO-REFORM OPINION WRITERS:

JOHANN HARI – consistently eloquent writer on drug law reform in the Independent. An archive of his writings on the issue is available here: www.johannhari.com/archive/index.php?subject=drugLegalisation

POLLY TOYNBEE- feted by left and right, the Guardian columnist and Transform supporter has produced some excellent opinion pieces on drug law reform, for example:
http://society.guardian.co.uk/drugsandalcohol/comment/0,,941745,00.html

SIMON JENKINS – Former editor of the Times, now

columnist for The Times, Sunday Times, Guardian, and Evening Standard, in all of which he regularly produces barnstorming opinion pieces, including this one: 'The really tough way to control drugs is to license them'
www.timesonline.co.uk/article/0,,2088-2472142,00

SIMON JENKINS AND POLLY TOYNBEE SPEAKING AT A TRANSFORM EVENT

MARY ANN SEIGHART - Assistant editor of the Times and outspoken supporter of reform. For example: 'Why we should medicalise not criminalise'
www.timesonline.co.uk/article/0,,1071-2501856,00

For more links to pro reform opinion writers visit the Transform quote archive
http://www.tdpf.org.uk/MediaNews_Reform_supporters_opinionformers.htm

....AND SOME ANTI-REFORM / PROHIBITIONIST ADVOCATE OPINION WRITERS

There are others, but the three below are arguably the highest-profile and most outspoken ultra-prohibitionist opinion writers in the UK. They have a lot in common and all are superb polemicists. Well worth reading as a way of getting to grips with the rhetoric of ideological prohibition (To note: the author of this guide has publicly debated both Phillips and Hitchens - and won on audience votes both times).

MELANIE PHILLIPS - The most vocal anti-drug law reform writer of the reactionary right-leaning opinion writers (currently working for the Daily Mail). She advocates using the criminal justice system to enforce personal morality and is passionately anti-legalisation/law reform, characterising the drug reform movement as a sinister elite dedicated to destroying the fabric of society. In many respects a brilliantly convincing prohibitionist for certain audiences, she takes spectacular liberties with the scientific and factual basis for her arguments.
www.melaniephillips.com/

PETER HITCHENS - Another barnstorming Daily Mail Columnist. In his (apparently self-edited) Wikipedia entry his views on drugs are described thus: "He argues that the law's active disapproval of drug taking is an essential counterweight to the "pro-drug propaganda" of popular culture. He considers attempts to combat drug use by restricting supply and persecuting dealers, futile, if possession and use are not punished as well. He answers claims that the "War on Drugs" has failed by suggesting that there has been no serious war on drugs for many years. Hitchens believes that the approach, known as "harm reduction", is defeatist and counter-productive." . An example of his work:
http://hitchensblog.mailonsunday.co.uk/2006/05/next_statefunde

SIMON HEFFER - A Daily Telegraph editor and outspoken in a simiarly prohibitionist vein to Phillips and Hitchens, though, if possible, even more confrontational: for example, from the linked article below:"Happy though the thought is, we cannot take 6,000 drugs dealers out on to a piece of waste ground and shoot them in the back of the head" www.telegraph.co.uk/opinion/main.jhtml?xml=/opinion/2006/12/13/do1301.xml

APPENDIX:

USING COMMON GROUND TO CRITIQUE PROHIBITION AND MAKE THE CASE FOR LEGALISATION AND REGULATION.

The table below uses the common ground principles and aims outlined in chapter 2 to provide a summary of the main arguments against prohibition and in favour of regulatory alternatives.

PROBLEMS WITH PROHIBITION	BENEFITS OF LEGAL REGULATION
TO MINIMISE PROBLEMATIC DRUG USE AND RELATED HEALTH HARMS, INCLUDING DRUG RELATED DEATHS	
• Problematic use and related harm has risen dramatically under prohibition. • Problem drug users, often the most vulnerable, excluded and needy members of society, are demonised and stigmatised by the criminal justice approach. It is totally unsuited to responding to their needs and helping them rebuild their lives. • Counterproductive enforcement spending diverts limited drug policy budgets away from where they can be more effectively spent on treatment and rehabilitation.	• The harm maximising effects of prohibition would largely be removed creating an environment in which more effective treatment, education and harm minimisation programmes could evolve, funded by redirected enforcement spending. • Problem users will benefit from support, not punishment and further marginalisation.

<table>
<tr><th>PROBLEMS WITH PROHIBITION</th><th>BENEFITS OF LEGAL REGULATION</th></tr>
<tr><td colspan="2">TO MINIMISE PROBLEMATIC DRUG USE AND RELATED HEALTH HARMS, INCLUDING DRUG RELATED DEATHS</td></tr>
<tr><td>• Prohibition focuses policy on combating the drugs themselves, and obscures the fact that problematic use is primarily a symptom of social deprivation. Only by addressing these underlying causes can problematic use be reduced in the long term – this is not a problem that can be solved by the criminal justice system.</td><td>• Numbers of drug related deaths would drop dramatically. Dependent users would no longer have to face the risks of impure street drugs and blood borne diseases including HIV and hepatitis.

• Policy makers could focus on addressing the social issues that underly most problematic drug use.</td></tr>
<tr><td colspan="2">TO MINIMISE CRIMINAL ACTIVITY ASSOCIATED WITH THE PRODUCTION AND SUPPLY AND USE OF DRUGS
TO MINIMISE DISORDER, VIOLENCE AND SOCIAL NUISANCE RELATED TO DRUG USE</td></tr>
<tr><td>• Prohibition actively stimulates crime at all scales[23].

• Recent Home Office research into the social and economic impact of Class A drugs in the UK estimated the costs in 2000 at between £10.1 and £17.4 billion. 88% of this total is the costs of drug-related crime, graphically illustrating how the costs of drug misuse itself are eclipsed by the far greater costs of crime created by prohibition[24].

• The reason that a relatively small number of dependent users of illegal drugs commit an enormous amount of crime whilst huge numbers of dependent users of legal or prescription drugs do not is essentially a matter of economics: illegal drugs are expensive, legal drugs are not.</td><td>• Legally regulated supplies of heroin and cocaine – on prescription or at prices that do not necessitate fundraising-related offending – have the potential to immediately reduce property crime committed by individual users by as much as a half (an effect observed with heroin prescribing projects in cities across Europe [20]).

• Simultaneously, most street prostitution and street dealing would disappear and there would be significant reductions in turf wars, gang violence and gun crime.

• With illegal drug markets dismantled, millions of drug users no longer criminalised, and dependent users no longer forced into offending to support a habit, a huge resource burden will be lifted from the entire criminal justice system, from police and customs, through to the courts, prisons and probation services.</td></tr>
</table>

PROBLEMS WITH PROHIBITION	BENEFITS OF LEGAL REGULATION
TO MINIMISE CRIMINAL ACTIVITY ASSOCIATED WITH THE PRODUCTION AND SUPPLY AND USE OF DRUGS TO MINIMISE DISORDER, VIOLENCE AND SOCIAL NUISANCE RELATED TO DRUG USE	
• A Number 10 Downing St Strategy Unit report in 2003 similarly estimated the crime costs of crime to support Class A drug habits to be £20 billion a year[12]. • In the wider world illegal drug profits are fuelling criminal activity on a huge scale, as well as funding corruption, conflict and terrorism in already unstable regions such as Colombia and Afghanistan.	• The largest single profit opportunity for organised crime would evaporate, and with it the largest single source of police corruption. • With major illegal drug markets dismantled, millions of drug users no longer criminalised, and dependent users no longer forced into offending to support a habit, a huge resource burden will be lifted from the entire criminal justice system, from police and customs, through to the courts, prisons and probation services. • Another obvious knock on effect of the dramatic drop in crime would be a huge reduction in the non-violent prison population. The prison population would quickly fall by between a third and a half, ending the funding and overcrowding crisis.
TO MINIMISE DRUG RELATED HARM TO VULNERABLE GROUPS, YOUNG PEOPLE AND FAMILIES	
• Prohibition not only increases harms for drug users, the majority of whom are young people, but also creates new harms associated with violent illegal markets and it is the young and vulnerable who bear the brunt of these harm. • Young people are on the front line of the drug war and constitute the majority of its 'collateral damage' in the UK and around the world	• Young people would be able – and more likely – to access drug services without the threat of criminality.

PROBLEMS WITH PROHIBITION	BENEFITS OF LEGAL REGULATION
TO MINIMISE DRUG RELATED HARM TO VULNERABLE GROUPS, YOUNG PEOPLE AND FAMILIES	
• The young are the most frequent victims of drug related crime and violence, both in the UK and in producer and transit countries such as Colombia and Jamaica. • Prohibition actively puts the young and vulnerable in harm's way – literally and metaphorically - as they are caught in the crossfire of the drug war.	• A more consistent, believable and effective message on the dangers of all drugs could be put across through appropriate public education channels – rather than using law enforcement as a primary educational tool.
TO ENSURE ADEQUATE PROVISION OF SUPPORT AND DRUG TREATMENT FOR PEOPLE SEEKING HELP	
• The criminal justice system is not the appropriate arena for addressing problematic drug use. • Outcomes for criminal justice administered treatment are extremely poor[25]. • A criminal justice oriented policy directs resources away from potentially effective education, prevention and treatment services, into enforcement that is demonstrably both ineffective and actively counterproductive.	• Drug services would no longer have to use the criminal justice system as a primary point of entry. Their work could be defined by public health indicators rather than crime reduction measures and the overt politicisation of the populist law and order agenda. Treatment decisions would be made by doctors and treatment professionals and not shaped by politicians or interference from the criminal justice system. • The 'peace dividend' from ending the 'drug war' could easily fund the necessary expansion of services.

PROBLEMS WITH PROHIBITION	BENEFITS OF LEGAL REGULATION
DRUG POLICY SHOULD SEEK TO REDUCE DRUG RELATED HARM	
• Prohibition maximises harms associated with drug use and creates new harms associated with the illegal market. Introducing harm reduction measures within the existing harm maximising prohibitionist framework is an exercise in futility.	• Policy would be based on harm reduction principles[26].
DRUG POLICY IS PRIMARILY A PUBLIC HEALTH ISSUE	
• Under prohibition, drug policy has become predominantly a criminal justice issue; a policy experiment and anomaly within the health arena that has no precedent and has had disastrous outcomes.	• With public health agencies taking the lead in policy development and implementation this principle would become practice rather than just an aspiration. The counterproductive and distorting influence of ideological crusades for a drug free society would be removed.
DRUG POLICY SHOULD BE BASED ON EVIDENCE OF EFFECTIVENESS	
• Prohibition is currently an evidence free zone that has required a huge propaganda exercise and decades of distorted and misrepresented statistics to maintain it. • Policy outcomes are not evaluated against meaningful indicators, leading to entrenchment of systemic failure, and unresponsiveness to changing circumstances over the past 40 years.	• Freed from the shackles of ideological prohibitionist dogma and populist law and order politics, policy would be able to develop based on sound science and evidence of effectiveness. • Policy outcomes would be able to be rigorously evaluated against meaningful indicators to demonstrate effectiveness. Policy can then evolve based on the success or failure of different approaches.

<table>
<tr><th>PROBLEMS WITH PROHIBITION</th><th>BENEFITS OF LEGAL REGULATION</th></tr>
<tr><td colspan="2">DRUG POLICY SHOULD OFFER GOOD VALUE FOR MONEY</td></tr>
<tr><td>• The 'war on drugs' has been a ruinous waste of billions of pounds of taxpayers' money for generations. Not only is it hugely expensive, with outcomes that are the exact opposite of its stated aims, but it actually creates secondary costs – in public health harms and crime creation.

• Prohibition ensures that the profits from an ever-expanding multi billion pound market are untaxed and accrue exclusively to criminal networks and gangsters.

• Drug enforcement spending has never been subject to an independent cost benefit analysis, properly evaluated or audited against meaningful indicators.</td><td>• Billions of pounds currently wasted enforcing prohibition and dealing with its catastrophic fallout would be saved. This 'peace dividend' from ending the drug war would be freed up for other criminal justice programmes. Funds could be redirected into drug treatment and education, or longer-term investment in reducing the social deprivation underlying most problematic drug use: a post-drug war 'Marshall Plan'.

• The illegal drug market in the UK is estimated to be worth at least £6 billion a year. Globally it turns over £300 billion a year[28]. Regulating and taxing this market would, as with alcohol and tobacco, create potentially significant revenues for the Treasury, as well as creating the opportunity to control prices.</td></tr>
<tr><td colspan="2">ALL DRUGS ARE POTENTIALLY DANGEROUS, AND ALL DRUG USE IS INTRINSICALLY RISKY</td></tr>
<tr><td>• Illegal production and supply of drugs increases risks associated with their use.</td><td>• The additional dangers of unknown strength and purity that are created by illegal production and supply would be removed.

• All drugs could at last have health warnings, dosage and safety information on the packaging. Further information could be available at point of sale or through better funded public health education.</td></tr>
</table>

PROBLEMS WITH PROHIBITION	BENEFITS OF LEGAL REGULATION
DOMESTIC AND INTERNATIONAL DRUG POLICY SHOULD FOSTER PEACE, GOOD GOVERNANCE, ECONOMIC STABILITY AND DEVELOPMENT	
• National sovereignty is undermined by the inflexibility of the UN drug conventions; entire avenues of policy development are closed for reasons of outdated drug war ideology and its entrenched legal structures – not evidence of effectiveness. • The world has changed dramatically since the 1950s when the UN drug conventions were drafted. They are hopelessly outdated and irrelevant to contemporary society. • Billions in illegal drug profits are used to corrupt all levels of police, judiciary and government in key drug production and transit countries – dramatically undermining their social, political and economic development prospects.	• States would be free to make democratic decisions about how they control and regulate drugs within their borders. • Policy could respond to changing circumstances. • The corrupting and destabilising influence of illegal drug profits would be removed.
POLICY SHOULD BE COMPATIBLE WITH DOMESTIC AND INTERNATIONAL HUMAN RIGHTS LEGISLATION	
• Only a few decades ago problematic drug users were treated in the UK for what they were – vulnerable people in need of help. Prohibition turns the majority of those without substantial private means into criminal outcasts, exacerbating social exclusion and throwing yet more obstacles in the way of achieving employment, housing, personal finance, and a generally productive and healthy life.	• Civil and human rights abuses could no longer be perpetrated under the banner of the drugs war.

PROBLEMS WITH PROHIBITION	BENEFITS OF LEGAL REGULATION
POLICY SHOULD BE COMPATIBLE WITH DOMESTIC AND INTERNATIONAL HUMAN RIGHTS LEGISLATION	
• Millions of otherwise law abiding individuals are being criminalised in a way that is arbitrary, unjust, and incompatible with the European Charter of Human Rights now incorporated into UK law. • There is widespread use of the death penalty for drug offences in violation of the UN Charter of Human Rights. China routinely celebrates UN world anti-drugs day with mass executions of drug offenders, 64 being executed on June 27th 2002, up from 54 the previous year[28]. Over 2000 people died during Thailand's drug 'crackdown' launched in 2002, many thought to be extra-judicial police executions[29]. • An estimated 2 million people are imprisoned globally for drug offences, one quarter of the total prison population. This places a huge financial and human cost on society with little evidence of any benefits. • Indigenous cultures in some producer countries that have long traditions of medical and ceremonial uses of local drug crops (coca, opium and cannabis) have come under attack through the criminalisation of traditional practices. • It is invariably the weakest links in the illegal drug chain (peasant growers, drug 'mules', and users) who feel the greatest impact of drug enforcement. Serious criminals have the resources to evade legal consequences and bargaining power as informants if they are caught.	• The threat of criminalisation and inprisonment would be lifted from millions of otherwise law abiding citizens. • The arbitrary and illegal use of the death penalty for non violent drug offences would end. • Indigenous cultures, traditional practices and marginalised, impoverished and vulnerable peoples would no longer be threatened by drug war policing and military interventions.

NOTES AND REFERENCES

[1] History of prohibition timeline: www.tdpf.org.uk/Policy_Timeline

[2] The other key beneficiaries being organised crime

[3] See the Transform website links page for extensive listing of drug policy and law reform organisations around the world

[4] 'Room for Manoeuvre: Overview of comparative legal research into national drug laws of France, Germany, Italy, Spain, the Netherlands and Sweden and their relation to three international drugs conventions' Nicholas Dorn, Alison Jamieson. Drugscope 2000 www.ahrn.net/library_upload/uploadfile/manoeuvre.pdf

[5] FAQ on prohibition: www.tdpf.org.uk/AboutUs_FAQ.htm#_prohibition

[6] Archive of quotes from supporters of reform: www.tdpf.org.uk/MediaNews_Reform_supporters

[7] 'Attitudes to Drug Policy and Drug Laws: A review of the international evidence' Dr Russell Newcombe 2004 http://www.tdpf.org.uk/newcombe2004.pdf

[8] 2003 Alcohol harm reduction strategy: www.cabinetoffice.gov.uk/strategy/downloads/su/alcohol/pdf/CabOffce%20AlcoholHar.pdf

[9] 'The drug prohibition church and the adventure of reformation' Peter Cohen. International Journal of Drug Policy, Volume 14, Issue 2, April 2003, pp. 213-215. http://www.cedro-uva.org/lib/cohen.church.html

[10] Transform fact research guide to enforcement expenditure: www.tdpf.org.uk/MediaNews_FactResearchGuide_EnforcementExpenditure

[11] Advisory Council on the Misuse of Drugs (ACMD) report 'Pathways to Problems' 2006

[12] No 10 Strategy Unit drugs report 2003: www.tdpf.org.uk/Policy_General_Strategy_Unit_Drugs_Report_phase_1.

[13] For more discussion on enforcement and deterrence see the Transform briefing on drug classification: http://www.tdpf.org.uk/Policy_General_Drug_Classification.htm , and this post on the Transform blog: http://transform-drugs.blogspot.com/2006/10/classification-and-deterrence-wheres.html

[14] The EU European Monitoring Centre for Drugs and Drug Addiction (EMCDDA)produces and annual report and a variety of other statistical information comparing drug use across Europe, based on national reporting: www.emcdda.europa.eu

[15] Science and Technology Select Committee 2006 report on drug classification : www.publications.parliament.uk/pa/cm200506/cmselect/cmsctech/1031/103102.htm

[16] There is a fascinating exploration of the prohibitionist insecurity in the US Drug Enforcement Agency's 'speaking out against drug legalization' website: www.usdoj.gov/dea/demand/speakout/index.html, which, for the record, is comprehensively debunked here: www.druglibrary.org/schaffer/dea/pubs/legaliz/contents.htm

[17] That alcohol and tobacco would be classified

as A/B were they illegal has recently been pointed out by the Home Affairs Select Committee (drugs report 2002 – see: ref 19), The Science and Technology Select Committee (drug classification report 2006), and even the Government appointed Advisory Council on the Misuse of Drugs ('pathways to problems' report 2006) – which is responsible for making recommendations to Government on drug classification.

[18] 'From Soft drink to Hard Drug; A Snapshop History of Coca, Cocaine and Crack' Mike Jay www.tdpf.org.uk/Policy_General_Cocaine_MJay.htm

[19] Home Affairs Select Committee Report 'The Government's Drug Policy: is it working?' 2002 www.tdpf.org.uk/Parliament_KeyReports.htm#hasc

[20] 'Prescribing heroin: what is the evidence?' Joseph Rowntree Foundation 2003 www.jrf.org.uk/knowledge/findings/socialpolicy/943.asp

[21] Discussion of drug law reform and the UN conventions: www.wiredinitiative.com/pdf/DBT_QandA.pdf

[22] Transform fact research guide to the size of the illegal drug market: www.tdpf.org.uk/MediaNews_FactResearchGuide_SizeOfTheDrugMarket

[23] For more discussion see 'Drugs and Crime – the link is prohibition' briefing here: http://www.tdpf.org.uk/Policy_Crime_DrugsandCrime-TheLinkisProhibition.htm

[24] Christine Godfrey et al (2002) – 'The economic and social costs of Class A drug use in England and Wales, 2000' www.homeoffice.gov.uk/rds/pdfs2/hors249.pdf (Note: this research was updated in 2006, see: http://www.homeoffice.gov.uk/rds/pdfs06/rdsolr1606.pdf)

[25] See National Audit Office 2004 on Drug Treatment and Testing Orders: www.nao.org.uk/pn/03-04/0304366.htm

[26] Definition of harm reduction from the UK Harm Reduction Alliance: www.ukhra.org/harm_reduction_definition.html

[27] Transform fact research guide to the size of the drug market: www.tdpf.org.uk/MediaNews_FactResearchGuide_SizeOfTheDrugMarket

[28] CNN news report: www.cnn.com/2001/WORLD/asi apcf/east/06/26/china.drugs/

[29] Amnesty International report www.amnesty.org/wire.nsf/May2003/Thailand

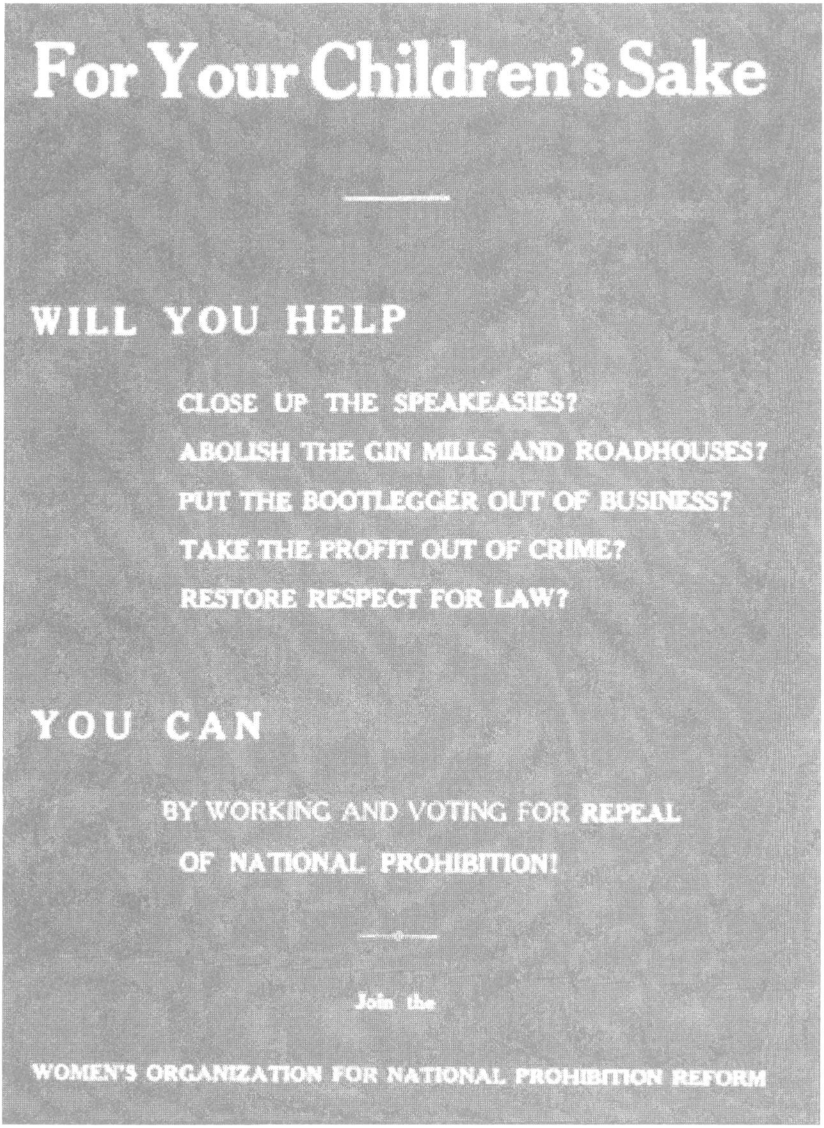

1920'S US ANTI PROHIBITION POSTER

TRANSFORM
DRUG POLICY FOUNDATION

Transform Drug Policy Foundation, Easton Business Centre, Felix Road, Bristol BS5 0HE.
Tel: 0117 941 5810.
Email: info@tdpf.org.uk
Web: www.tdpf.org.uk

Transform Drug Policy Foundation is a Registered Charity no.1100518 and Limited Company no.4862177